T0339712

Cambridge Elements ≡

Elements in Politics and Society in Southeast Asia
edited by
Edward Aspinall
Australian National University
Meredith L. Weiss
University at Albany, SUNY

URBAN DEVELOPMENT IN SOUTHEAST ASIA

Rita Padawangi

Singapore University of Social Sciences

CAMBRIDGE
UNIVERSITY PRESS

CAMBRIDGE
UNIVERSITY PRESS

University Printing House, Cambridge CB2 8BS, United Kingdom

One Liberty Plaza, 20th Floor, New York, NY 10006, USA

477 Williamstown Road, Port Melbourne, VIC 3207, Australia

314–321, 3rd Floor, Plot 3, Splendor Forum, Jasola District Centre, New Delhi – 110025, India

103 Penang Road, #05–06/07, Visioncrest Commercial, Singapore 238467

Cambridge University Press is part of the University of Cambridge.

It furthers the University's mission by disseminating knowledge in the pursuit of education, learning, and research at the highest international levels of excellence.

www.cambridge.org
Information on this title: www.cambridge.org/9781108705608
DOI: 10.1017/9781108669108

© Rita Padawangi 2022

First published 2022

A catalogue record for this publication is available from the British Library.

ISBN 978-1-108-70560-8 Paperback
ISSN 2515-2998 (online)
ISSN 2515-298X (print)

Urban Development in Southeast Asia

Elements in Politics and Society in Southeast Asia

DOI: 10.1017/9781108669108
First published online: June 2022

Rita Padawangi
Singapore University of Social Sciences
Author for correspondence: Rita Padawangi, ritapadawangi@suss.edu.sg

Abstract: Urbanization as a process is rife with inequality, in Southeast Asia as anywhere else, but resistance and contestation persist on the ground. This Element sets out to achieve three goals: 1) to examine the political nature of urban development; 2) to scrutinize the implications of power inequality in urban development discussions; and 3) to highlight topical and methodological contributions to urban studies from Southeast Asia. The key to a robust understanding is groundedness: knowledge about the everyday realities of urban life that are hard to see on the surface but dominate how the city functions, with particular attention to human agency and the political life of marginalized groups. Ignoring politics in research on urbanization essentially perpetuates the power inequities in urban development; this Element thus focuses not just on Southeast Asian cities and urbanization per se but also on critical perspectives on patterns and processes in their development.

Keywords: urban development, cities, urban planning, urban politics, urbanization

This Element also has a video abstract: www.cambridge.org/padawangi

ISBNs: 9781108705608 (PB), 9781108669108 (OC)
ISSNs: 2515-2998 (online), 2515-298X (print)

Contents

1 The Politics of Urban Development in Southeast Asia

Why do we need to study urban development in Southeast Asia? Most of the world's population is now urban (UN-Habitat, 2017); rapid, widespread urbanization is not unique to Southeast Asia. Moreover, there has been plenty of research on various cities in this region, so why should we need more of it? I argue that studying urban development in Southeast Asia is important for at least two reasons: first, to contribute to larger conceptual understandings of urban development; and second, to shape a new vantage point that reconfigures the relationship between academia and planning practice in contested urban landscapes. In other words, we need to critically revisit the "what" and the "how" of studying cities, as well as the extent to which the "what" and "how" are connected, and Southeast Asia provides valuable examples with which to do so. Many cities in Southeast Asia remain subjected to prescribed best practices from elsewhere, a symptom of insufficient conceptual development from studies in and of this region to build a comprehensive and robust understanding of urbanization. We face an urgent need to reshape studies of urban development in Southeast Asia in light of the consequences of urbanization for everyday lived experiences.

What is it about Southeast Asia that has most influenced the shape of cities, urban life, and urbanization? Is there anything distinctive about urban development in Southeast Asia? Much of what we find in Southeast Asia is not distinct to this region. More than two decades ago, Howard Dick and Peter Rimmer warned that "any attempt to explain either the historical or contemporary urbanization of south-east Asia as a unique phenomenon is … doomed to absurdity" (1998: 2319). It was Terry McGee's concept of *desakota* (1991) – a mixed village-city, agricultural-urban landscape – as a distinctive urbanization pattern in the region that Dick and Rimmer (1998) viewed as a variation of urban sprawl that can be found elsewhere. To this day, *desakota* continues to be influential in studies of urbanization in developing countries, including in China and India. The expansion of the application of the concept beyond the region in which it emerged indicates that the phenomenon may not be distinctively Southeast Asian. Therefore, the key reason to study urban development in Southeast Asia is not to look for its distinctiveness. Rather, studying urban development in Southeast Asia is important for identifying patterns and processes of city life that are not sufficiently explained by existing theories and concepts.

Understanding the patterns and processes of Southeast Asia's urban development is part of a larger effort to build knowledge about cities, urban life, and urbanization. The range of studies of urban development in Southeast Asia today reflects Margit Mayer's concerns in her observation of urban studies in developing regions of the world: There are many case studies of local efforts and comparative analyses of various issues – such as poverty, social housing, evictions, and resistance movements – but there is not yet a comprehensive picture out of such a "fragmented map of . . . hard-fought contestations" (2020: 45). However rich the literature on Southeast Asia, like studies of urbanization elsewhere it warrants a refocus, given rapidly changing realities on the ground and the need to better align academic perspectives, planners' assumptions, and lived experiences.

A major challenge in refocusing studies of urban development is the emphasis on pragmatism in research, as urbanization has become the world's recipe for economic growth. Such a pragmatic focus on delivering bread-and-butter issues obscures the need for critical analysis of political power inequalities inherent in development strategies. In other words, the ends of developments justify the means, and scholars are caught in this process. These urbanizations assume certain images of a desirable future, to be achieved through prescribed strategies for development. The problem with these future images is that, while they are normative in terms of to where and how to progress, they come with technocratic and investment-driven narratives that exacerbate power inequalities in urban development (Ghertner, 2010; Harms, 2012; Padawangi, 2018c). In a socially fragmented landscape with increasing complexities cultivated over several decades of rapid urbanization, urban development becomes an arena in which "progress" for some comes at a cost of displacement of others, often the socially and economically marginal.

Yet not only are urbanizing landscapes of Southeast Asia places of social marginalization and environmental destruction in the name of development, but they also present alternatives to the state's official narratives. These alternatives are indicative of actions on the ground that reflect communities' human agency and political life. Active participation of disenfranchised communities in urban development opens avenues to understanding cities, urban life, and urbaniza-tion as political terrain on which socially and politically active communal enclaves coexist with top-down planners.

By proposing a new vantage point that critically examines urban develop-ment, this Element helps to meet this important need for a deeper understanding of urbanization, one that captures how power inequalities manifest materially in urban spaces. First and foremost, this Element fully recognizes that urban development is political, and therefore studying urban development must be critical. This recognition is key to shaping one's perspective on urban develop-ment and consequently influences the methods one selects. The methods that scholars and practitioners adopt – whether ground-up or top-down – ultimately structure the ability of urban development to address core challenges of social justice and environmental justice in real-life settings. Therefore, the choice of perspective is not just "academic" but has real implications for the future of cities in Southeast Asia.

1.1 Southeast Asia as a Postcolonial Region

To study Southeast Asia's urban development, the extent of its complexities, and its contradictions, one must understand the scope of the region itself. Mostly emerging in its current geopolitical form after World War II and decolonization, Southeast Asia is a relatively "new" region in the field of urban studies, and studies on urban development here grew along with the increasing role of the region in the world economy (Rimmer & Dick, 2019). Reflecting the fact that Southeast Asia is a postcolonial region, thus far its urban development has two contradictory realities: first, in extending colonial systems; and second, as stages for nationalist projects.

Urban development as an extension of colonial systems comes from the formation of Southeast Asia's nation-states as "by-products" of colonial states (Anderson, 1983) in terms of their categories and territories, as well as the "cultural" positions of the residents as postcolonial subjects. Colonial urban planning was a tool to sustain order, contain disorder, and modernize as the "rational choice" to achieve the public good, but it did so to "incorporate colonies into the capitalist world economy" (Kusno, 2017a: 219; Yeoh, 1996). Such objectives continue in the postcolonial era, as urban planning applies technocratic approaches to gear cities to become gateways for global capitalism. Postcolonial urban planning extends to more all-encompassing scales, however, as contemporary capitalism requires participation of the whole landscape in the market economy (Yeoh, 1996).

We see the second frame, of urban development to showcase nationalism, in modern buildings and monumental projects in postcolonial times. Newly independent countries often rely on these buildings and projects to paint an image of a nation free of colonial subordination, but their now-sovereign leaders continue to preserve some legacies of the colonial era (Kusno, 2017b: 231). These monumental projects appear in official maps, but self-built, semi-autonomous enclaves do not appear in detail. In the colonial era, such semi-autonomous enclaves functioned as spaces for the Indigenous population but also contained those populations, albeit allowing a degree of self-governance. In the postcolonial era, these enclaves continue to absorb populations and buffer the government's incapacity to provide affordable housing, but they continue to be underrepresented in cities' official maps, which instead highlight flagship projects and larger buildings. Moreover, their capacity for autonomy has declined as subsequent regulations and structural transformations have brought more spaces into the capitalist economy. Over time, urban development planning has tended increasingly in favor of technocratic planning, which provides spatial engineering tools for societal control and discipline to support economic growth, in the name of national progress.

These two contradictory realities share a core attribute: both are top-down. Nonetheless, contestation and negotiation also shape the city and urbanization processes in Southeast Asia, not just overarching control of the state. In her seminal work *Contesting Space in Colonial Singapore*, Brenda Yeoh (1996) points to the importance of examining the role of urban actors in these challenges. In other words, although urban development seems to be a rational-technocratic vehicle to achieve public good, what gets built is a result of political processes, and it is important to understand these political processes to be able to obtain a comprehensive view of the seemingly fragmented city. This is a difficult terrain to navigate because it requires mapping political actors and linkages onto the built environment. Yet this navigation is necessary to allow in-depth understanding of urban development dynamics in Southeast Asia. An assumption of a linear progression of development is problematic, as the evolution of cities through various historical eras reflects a mix of continuity and discontinuity in urban systems. Such a situation requires scholars to focus on "distinctions between what is residual and tenacious, what is dominant but hard to see, and ... what is emergent in today's imperial formations – and critically resurgent in responses to them" (Stoler, 2008: 211).

1.2 Urban Development as Power Contestations

Urban development in Southeast Asia is a manifestation of power contestations. Property developers have emerged as dominant actors in the making of urban spaces in Southeast Asia, following the ascendancy of technocratic approaches and investment-driven planning in decades of postcolonial industrialization. Although several countries – namely Indonesia, the Philippines, and, to a certain extent, Thailand and Myanmar (before the latter's military coup in 2021) – have undergone waves of democratization in the late twentieth and early twenty-first centuries, even the democratization process "did not sufficiently address the urban development course that allowed over-corporatization of urban spaces" (Padawangi, 2014: 47).

The continued hegemony of technocratic planning in global-capitalism-plugged economies has converted built environments into spaces that celebrate consensus while stigmatizing dissent. Beautiful, tidy landscapes embody aspirations for a "good city." For instance, Erik Harms (2012) observes in Ho Chi Minh City the extent to which those who were displaced by city beautification projects had internalized aspirations for neatly manicured spaces and therefore resigned themselves to the fate of being evicted. Beautification is part of many cities' urban development practices, intended to project their competitiveness in the globalizing economy. Those projects pursue convenience and beautiful landscapes at all cost, as prescriptive strategies to facilitate economic growth. When urban spaces become economic assets, the concept of public space fades, as political discussions in such spaces are seen as obstacles to safe orderliness (Bayat, 2012). Forced displacements for these projects become pragmatic decisions, taken to implement projects framed as necessary interventions to modernize the city.

The increasing implementation of these neoliberal practices as "the new orthodoxy within urban governance" (Paddison, 2009: 8) raises questions regarding the maintenance of political spaces within rapidly urbanizing Southeast Asia. When contemporary urban development and governance regimes constrain the political spaces that societies have relied upon thus far to participate in the making of cities and urban life in Southeast Asia, what are the consequences for urban development trajectories in the region? The question also applies the other way around: What are the consequences of these urban development trajectories for politics in the region? And to what extent do scholars take those consequences into account in assessing urban spaces, projects, and governance?

1.3 Structure of the Element

This Element dissects patterns and processes of urbanization in Southeast Asia to demonstrate that these have always been political and to chart an agenda for future studies of urban development. Section 2 follows historical trails to analyze aspects of urban planning in the past that still characterize Southeast Asia's urban development in the present. The discussion continues in Section 3 by dispelling the "lack of planning" myth as a stereotype of urbanization in Southeast Asia. The section's emphasis on the mismatch between urban plans, implementation, and everyday life on the ground, which bears the consequences of injustices that urban development exacerbates, leads to Section 4, on the "how" of studying urban development. Since top-down perspectives in practice are limited in their ability to address injustices, studies of urban development require groundedness for a more complete picture of power inequalities and their impacts on urban life. This section examines innovative research methods and approaches to connect scales from the micro to the macro and to critically question the limits of administrative boundaries. It should no longer be acceptable to rely only on official data and formal channels, as such an approach obscures reality on the ground. Section 5 continues with the consequences of these approaches for understanding social and environmental justice in urban development. The discussion connects social and environmental issues with urban politics, in which stakeholders and the power inequalities among them have real impacts on lives and livelihoods and make the city a political stage in pursuit of (and against) justice.

Section 6, on the region's urban futures, discusses potentials and possibilities for Southeast Asia's cities and the study of them. This section covers aspirations for and imaginations of the future of the urban, from multiple perspectives. Given the misalignment of interests that the preceding section identifies, these perspectives from various urban development actors diverge, yielding fragmented visions of the city, notwithstanding points of convergence. As neoliberal government regimes constrain political spaces and present urban development as a series of pragmatic fixes for the built environment, aspirations for the future city take the shape of assemblages of imagined interventions that appear technical and still reflect the hegemony of technocratic planning in the city. Paying closer attention to the role of activism in directing urban futures, though, highlights the importance of observing alternative urban development programs and projects as counter-, yet inseparable, narratives to technocratic and investment-driven official ones. Such an emphasis recognizes the human agency that continues to shape cities and urban developments in Southeast Asia. Studies of urban development in Southeast Asia require clear awareness of power inequalities to avoid aggravating them. One challenge that lies immediately ahead is the availability of data to study and to conceptualize alternative development projects, and therefore the Element concludes with a call for engaged scholarship on urban development in Southeast Asia.

2 Historical "Debris" in Southeast Asia's Urban Development

Southeast Asia took shape as a geographical region in urban studies mostly after World War II as the countries involved underwent rapid industrialization. Yet urban development in Southeast Asia has a significantly longer history. This section presents urban development as an ongoing process that both dismantles and repurposes "debris" of the past (Stoler, 2008), not exactly in a linear progression but more through continuous power struggles among actors ranging from those who hold high political power to ordinary citizens. The built environment, as a result of (and as a record of) these processes, becomes a set of physical manifestations of the political nature of urban development.

2.1 From "Cosmic Centers" to "Nationalist Centers"

Historians and archaeologists have noted the existence of societies in the region with relatively diverse social and economic activities since the first millennium. Adding to this variation was trade, including within and among Southeast Asia, China, India, and Europe between the fifteenth and seventeenth centuries (Reid, 1993). Trade in commodities such as spices and wood spurred the growth of port cities and, consequently, urban centers in relation to these port economies. Islam and Christianity also grew in Southeast Asia during this period, which transformed the cities' religious, social, political, and cultural landscapes (Reid, 1993). Even prior to the fifteenth century, trade and cultural exchanges with China and India had played a role in Southeast Asia's commerce. Denys Lombard (1995) argues that Southeast Asia was not just a "crossroad" of two oceans and two continents but a lively region of trade with established Chinese networks, Muslim networks, and Christian networks within the region. Records of maritime trade missions to China's Song Dynasty show voyages as early as 947 AD, noting official trade missions from Srivijaya, Champa, Java, Brunei, and Cambodia, among others (Wade, 2012). Traces of urbanization and trade in the first millennium showed cultural influences from India; the existence of pre-Indianization towns, although possible, is still a subject of debate among archaeologists (Savage, 2019).

Although trade was important to the sustainability of Southeast Asia's kingdoms, cities in the region at the time connected functions of inter-kingdom trade with a "cosmic city" concept, in which the city became the ceremonial center, surrounded by the kingdom's agricultural lands (Savage, 2019). These cosmic cities collected agricultural surpluses and functioned as the political and cultural core of the kingdom, as the king was both the political and the spiritual leader. Urban plans revolved around this leadership, with the ceremonial ground, palace, and temple located at the center. This urban plan and societal structure were among the legacies of Indian religious influence in the region, dating back to the first millennium.

Parallels of the "cosmic city" concept can still be found in today's cities in Southeast Asia. They are not exactly similar, but the social, cultural, political, and physical constructions of cities and urban life in the region have not fully shed the "debris" of that history (Stoler, 2008). These expressions of political culture appear in the built environment, and assertions of power are apparent in cultural beliefs and practices (Anderson, 1983). National monuments and symbolic projects, such as the National Monument and the Miniature Park in Indonesia, are examples of how politicians ensure cities physically embody tropes of national symbols. The story of nation-building in Southeast Asia is often a story of urban development that is infused with the notion of an imagined community of the nation, oriented symbolically around the capital city.

But what about the technocratic side of cities that seems to disenchant societies from such cultural symbolism? In spite of its technicalities, postcolonial industrialization does not reduce symbolic orientation toward and around the capital city; rather, industrial development gradually infuses infrastructural projects as national symbols. Instead of making symbolism obsolete, the concentration of buildings, industries, and their related infrastructures have evolved to be the new face of nationalism. An observable practice of urban development as nation-building appears in the case of Singapore, where infrastructural projects for urban living have been integral parts of national pride. High-rise buildings and advanced transportation infrastructures as symbols of progress stand as orientations of aspired progress as national identity.

Singapore is currently the city with the highest per capita income in the region, and it is also a country that is officially "100 percent urbanized" (UN Population Division, 2018). Provision of basic infrastructure services such as water and public housing has illustrated the city-state's development as a sovereign nation with a government that is capable of providing services to the people. Yet Singapore's development is also one of urban expansion, as the "city" area used to be only the downtown area nearer to the port, governed by the municipal authority, while most of the main island and the smaller islands that surrounded it was rural, composed of various village settlements. Eventually most of these areas became residential neighborhoods to house the urbanized labor force, as the economy industrialized after its national independence. The city also annexed surrounding islands, reorienting the nation as a city-state rather than the sprawling archipelago of seventy small islands that it was prior to land reclamation. The story of Singapore's progress is a story of urban development, with expanding transportation services, housing provision, industrial parks, and a financial center. Capacity to deliver pragmatic results in Singapore's urban development is still an important source of political capital until today. Members of parliament campaign for elections based on their perceived ability to maintain cleanliness, build neighborhood centers, and administer other development projects.

Recent evolution of political life echoes the "cosmic city" concept as cities continue to function as political, economic, and cultural centers of power. In the case of Thailand as a constitutional monarchy, Bangkok as the capital city is also where the king is seated, and it continues to be the orientation of cultural, political, and religious symbolism. Nevertheless, Chiang Mai as an old cosmic center of Lanna Kingdom has now also become a center for the red shirt political camp vis-à-vis the yellow shirts in Bangkok. One might argue that the second-order city just happens to be the hometown of the opposition Shinawatra family, but Chiang Mai has a history of being the center of political power in northern Thailand, felt across continental Southeast Asia. Meanwhile, some nation-states in Southeast Asia have transitioned into democracies, but the centralization of economic activities in cities has made them fertile grounds to build political capital. Rodrigo Duterte of the Philippines and Joko Widodo of Indonesia are examples of contemporary politicians who capitalize on the legacy of the city as accumulation of power. Both contested for the presidency as local figures – problem-solving mayors of second-order cities – but have since built populist followings by marshaling the power of the center: they present themselves, like the capital cities from which they now govern, as the center and embodiment of the nation. In the case of Widodo, he served as governor of the capital city Jakarta for less than one term as a stepping stone toward seizing the presidential seat, garnering popular support through widely shared images of technocratic progress in the capital city. Duterte, on the other hand, relied on the claims of progress in Davao for his presidential campaign. Progress in second-order cities – ranging from basic needs fulfillment to ensuring the convenience of city living, safety, and security – serve to augment the political power of such national leaders to take over the center.

2.2 The "Debris" of the "Colonial City"

The historical political, social, and cultural debris that still shapes Southeast Asia's contemporary cities comes from various eras, but the one that has been most studied in relation to urban development is the European colonial era. Scholars have argued that the colonial era, in which trade intensified with imperial Europe, was a precursor to the immersion of cities into global capitalism (Yeoh, 1996). Although intercontinental trade preceded colonial forces' arrival in the region, what made this era distinct was the shift of power relations in urban development decisions. Political negotiations, conflicts, and the accumulation of wealth in the European colonies contributed to the shaping of racially diverse, yet unequal, societies through the development of infrastructure and the urban fabric.

The earliest colonial trace in the urban fabric in Southeast Asia was from the Portuguese in Melaka, starting with the arrival of their traders in 1511. Later on, some European colonies in the region had fortified towns, with the Europeans within the walls and others outside, reflecting segregation and fear of the local population. These forts were usually in port cities that were important for trade connections. Remains of these European forts still stand in several cities, such as Jakarta's Batavia and Manila's Intramuros. In cities without forts, the differentiation of European colonial sections from the rest of the city was still apparent in aspects of European engineering, such as infrastructure and building techniques. That spatial segregation reflected both racial and class inequality in urban life, as the wealth from intercontinental trade was unequally distributed.

However, it is too simplistic to assume that colonial-era urbanization only led to segregation, as there is historical evidence of integration in practice. Official planning documents might have designated specific ethnic quarters, but local acts of desegregation were possible. For example, under the Dutch colonial rule in Surabaya, *Wijkenstelsel* applied as an ethnicity-based zoning policy, coupled with the *Passenstelsel* policy that required members of the Chinese ethnic and other "foreign oriental" groups to obtain permits for travel outside their quarters. As restrictive as these policies might seem, their implementation was not so effective – as evidence of, for instance, intermarriage between prominent Chinese officials and Javanese royalty suggests (Sutherland, 1974). Furthermore, the designation of the *kampung* as the quarters for "other natives" of the city at the time allowed *kampung* in Surabaya to welcome new migrants without ethnic restrictions and to accommodate interethnic families (Perkasa, Padawangi & Farida, 2021). Although this does not automatically indicate seamless ethnic integration, the possibility of forming ethnically diverse neighborhoods despite the implementation of ethnic segregation regulations suggested common practices that might be hard to see if one only looked at official policies.

The misalignment between official policies and everyday lived realities indicated an assertion of human agency amidst bureaucratic control. There were also more open displays of challenge to the ruling powers in the colonial era, such as the resistance that led to the strike of Chinese businesses in Singapore against new legislation on political representation and municipal reform in the second half of the nineteenth century (Yeoh, 1996: 32–33). Even though there was an impression of relatively strong bureaucratic control of urban planning in Singapore in the hands of the municipal authority at the time, the bureaucratic management reflected power negotiations "more commonly articulated through strategies of evasion, non-compliance, and adjustment, or channelled through Asian leaders" (Yeoh, 1996: 67). This is not to suggest that colonial powers failed to influence urban development; in fact, the example of ethnic segregation illustrates how adherence to and ways around policies might coexist. Such incomplete alignment (and misalignments) between official policies and the spectrum of everyday lived realities continues to shape today's urban development in Southeast Asia.

At least three legacies of the colonial city still leave traces to date. The first is the increasing power of global trade in the urban economy. Rather than being places to collect agricultural surpluses as in the cosmic centers, cities became places to control the kinds of agricultural products to be delivered. The centrality of cities in postcolonial economies led to the exponential growth of their population and territory. Second, the colonial powers brought European infrastructure to the city, including to connect one city to another. The focus on sending raw materials and natural resources to the port drove the development of roads, railroads, and waterways to deliver goods. Such a city-centric economic model continued in many parts of Southeast Asia after colonial rule ended post–World War II, as Southeast Asia's early postcolonial economies quickly came to rely on manufacturing and export-oriented production. Third, the underlying aspirations of the post-independence city, imbued with nationalist ideals, bear traces of colonial planning and infrastructure. These expectations and standards have affected both policymakers and societies, resulting in a mix of nationalist sentiments and colonial debris that can also lead to double standards between denouncing colonialism in monumental projects and holding colonial systems in high esteem in infrastructure development projects (Kusno, 2017b). Academic research and publications on urbanization in Southeast Asia in the early postcolonial period also followed this pattern, largely drawing on "Western experiences of urbanization, foregrounding economic motivations for rural-urban migration" (Bunnell, Goh & Ng, 2019), which reinforced the image of the aspirational city in reference to the colonial, European, or Western world in general.

2.3 The "Debris" of . . . the "City"?

Cities remain centers of political and economic powers in Southeast Asia, but the contradictions between their increasingly expansionist developments – swallowing surrounding rural landscapes and absorbing migrants to support cities' roles in trades beyond immediate vicinities – and the continuing misalignment of official realities vis-à-vis everyday lived realities have consequences for the dynamic of urban life that ensues from such urbanization processes. While the term "city" by definition indicates the social, political, economic, and cultural organization of a group of people who reside in a particular geographical location, the magnitude of urbanization in Southeast Asia requires us to understand how possibly several ways of organizing the city may be functioning at the same time, at times in parallel, at other times complementing, and at some other times contradicting each other. It is difficult to fit such competing layers of urban life with how the city has been defined in literatures – for example, the Weberian understanding of the city as a place that features social institutions, political structure, rule of law, and market (Weber, 1921). When urban planning, which is a combination of those features, does not match realities on the ground, then institutions and structures might not be working. The question that might arise would be, is it possible that urban development does not shape cities? Or, worse, does contemporary urban development in Southeast Asia ruin cities? Are these urban development manifestations that we see in Southeast Asia really cities or just "debris" of "cities"?

Given the continuing, even increasing, importance of these political and economic centers in Southeast Asia, most likely what we are encountering is that we need new perspectives in defining cities as social-political-economic-cultural expressions of urban development. Therefore, rather than seeing these urban development expressions as debris of cities, seeing the impact of collisions between competing political and economic powers in driving urban developments of Southeast Asia is important in revising our understanding of what a "city" might be.

In postcolonial Southeast Asia, the role of cities has nevertheless become increasingly important for at least two reasons. First is the growth in the urban share of the population in national demographics, from 15.4 percent overall in Southeast Asia in 1950 to 41.8 percent in 2010 (ISEAS, 2009). The United Nations has projected a continuing increase in that share, to reach approximately 50 percent in 2025 (Figures 1 and 2). As such, cities have become ever more important for national governments, in terms of policymaking and to maintain public support.

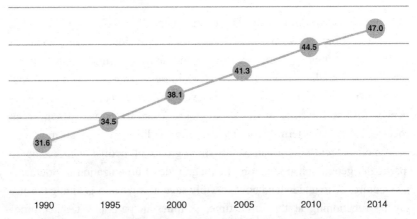

Figure 1 Proportion of urban population in Southeast Asia (%).
Data source: UN, 2014.

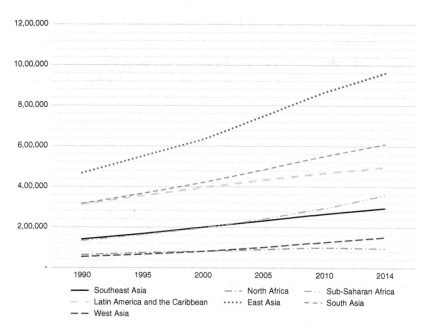

Figure 2 Urban population at mid-year by major area, in thousands.
Data source: UN, 2014.

The second reason is the paradigm of cities as engines of economic growth, advocated by international financing institutions that hold significant roles in infrastructure investments. Urban development has come to comprise a set of recipes for social and economic progress. All "developing" regions have trended toward an increasing urban population in recent decades, as urbanization has become an important indication of development. Cities, as showcases of progress, are also spaces of intersection between urban and national politics. This situation reconnects with the historical "debris" of both the "cosmic city" as a symbolic center of power and the infrastructural approach of the "colonial city." It is that mix that has led some cities in the region to become political stages and landscapes for populist politics, as politicians seek higher seats of power, and urban development to consist substantially of strategies in the pursuit of political power.

The fact of Southeast Asia's cities' social and economic importance in the development of postcolonial nation-states has coincided with the growing interconnectedness of the global capitalist economy. After the colonial era, in the second half of the twentieth century, manufacturing industries grew and became propellers of Southeast Asia's urban economies. During that period, the "New International Division of Labor" (NIDL), marked by "deep de-industrialization of the Fordist factory system in North America and Europe" and the shift of manufacturing industries to emerging economies, resulted in growing industrial complexes in various cities in Asia (Douglass & Jones, 2008: 26–27). These growing city-scale complexes constituted mega-urban regions (MURs) –networks of cities that were socially and economically interconnected. Most MURs in Southeast Asia were places where light industries such as garments and textiles grew to supply the global market, except in Malaysia where industries focused on electronics (Douglass & Jones, 2008; Warouw, 2019).

Current MURs in Southeast Asia, however, originated before industrialization in the late twentieth century, mostly as port cities in the colonial era. These port cities were mostly still under 1 million population in the 1960s, but their development to become centers of new industrializing economies brought exponential population growth, as shown by the example of the Jakarta MUR's population increase in Figure 3. Industries agglomerated at and around existing port cities as they offered optimal access to logistical, financial, and administrative services for export-oriented industrial products (Ortega, 2019). Special economic zones (SEZs) emerged around existing cities and have contributed to the expansion of mega-urban regions in the form of industrial parks or other large-scale urban developments, as spaces to attract foreign direct investment. These SEZs also connect foreign investors with local businesses and workers, which eventually creates the need for more commercial and residential space, leading to the mega-regionalization of urban development.

Mega-urban regions are both geographical linkages between local and global economies *and* sites of social and environmental inequalities. While attracting

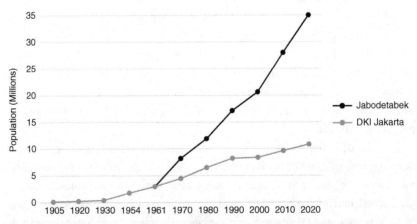

Figure 3 Population of Jakarta-Bogor-Depok-Bekasi metropolitan area (Jabodetabek) and DKI Jakarta.
Sources: Douglass & Jones, 2008; BPS Census, 2010; and Population Projection, 2020.

foreign direct investments, mega-urban regions, as concentrations of economic activities, also attract migrants. Migrants from rural areas, seeking jobs in big cities and in need of affordable housing, often must settle based on informal agreements in informal settlements (Ortega, 2019). Concurrently, expanding mega-urban regions consume land in the countryside adjacent to cities, often involving taking land away from peasants and traditional societies. These land acquisitions may or may not involve insufficient compensation, deception, and/ or use of force. The closeness between economic and political powers, as well as the role of politicians in these economic powerhouses of the country, often intensifies the process of converting land to investors' private ownership and allows special procedures that range from bypassing legal processes to prescription of special projects (Phuc, Zoomers & van Westen, 2015; Batubara et al., 2020). These conversions have social and environmental consequences beyond the transformations of livelihoods and landscapes that they bring, which will be discussed further in Section 5. Large-scale land-use change to facilitate industrial, commercial, and residential expansion without sufficient attention to environmental concerns has induced ecological degradation of soil, rivers, and the sea. The biggest mega-urban regions in Southeast Asia – Jakarta, Bangkok, Metro Manila, and Ho Chi Minh City – are suffering from land subsidence, mostly because of overdevelopment and over-extraction of groundwater. Some rivers in these regions have also degraded to the level of being biologically dead because of the pollution from industrial and residential waste, combined with deforestation upstream.

Attention to social inequalities and environmental degradation in these regions has become imperative in order to increase Southeast Asia's livability (Douglass & Jones, 2008), as it is likely that mega-urban regions will continue to be economic and population centers for some time. Urban planning scholars have called for innovative structures to govern mega-urban regions, particularly to allow more coordinated planning across multiple local government areas that are socially, economically, and environmentally interconnected. Currently, most of the largest mega-urban regions have metropolitan authorities that function as coordinating and governing bodies, but the authority of such bodies may still be limited in monitoring and implementing regional regulations. The absence of such coordinated governance structures in these MURs is another tempting entry point that presume that urban development may not build cities as coherent institutions; rather, it ruins cities, and what we are seeing now are fragmented debris of social, cultural, political, and legalistic institutions that are supposed to shape cities. However, social and environmental concerns elevate the urgency of having innovative governance structures to coordinate MURs. Hence, the ability to reconfigure parallel social, political, economic, and cultural processes to reduce the impact of their collisions on social and environmental realities – in other words, having social and environmental justice perspectives – is important as an objective in studying cities and urban development, as we will see in more detail in Section 5.

2.4 Learning from History

Even as many cities and urban regions in Southeast Asia keep, hide, or repurpose these layers of historical "debris," one connecting trend throughout history has been the legacy of negotiation and struggle over urban policies and spaces. Regardless of whether points of contestation were officially recorded, they influenced the course of urban development and their impacts, as well as traces that remained in lived realities have made it possible to identify them.

In today's context, urban areas have continued to accumulate economic and social activities, be these local, global, or somewhere in between. Exponential growth of the population and economy of cities after World War II resulted in pressures on cities' existing infrastructure. As a result, demands for infrastructure improvements also grew exponentially, while plans and reality have historically tended to misalign. Urban transformations in Southeast Asia often outpace the capacity of planners and city managers to be able to connect realities on the ground with official policies (Yap, 2019). Issues such as traffic jams, river pollution, and lack of green areas have become common problems in big cities such as Jakarta, Manila, and Bangkok. Singapore is often seen as an outlier among Southeast Asia's cities for its relatively advanced infrastructural developments and economic system, but to achieve that level the city has relied on heavy interventions in existing urban landscapes. In many instances, such interventions completely uprooted the population from existing settlements to make way for new developments; this phenomenon could be seen as clearing one set of historical "debris" to make way for repurposing others.

City governments' inabilities to meet demands for infrastructure and services in time compel societies to find their own ways to provide for household and shared community needs (Yap & Thuzar, 2012). "Informal" housing is an example of how such a dynamic materializes, in the context of a lack of affordable housing; other examples relate to provision of other goods and public services. As these provisions are usually ground-up or incremental, their physical appearance may be less homogenous than is the case for state-provided alternatives, and they may come across as "unplanned." In such settings, relations and linkages across different settlements may be based on compromises between two or more communities and the availability of space, and the spaces that are constructed may continue to transform according to emerging needs in the community. They may be experimental and temporary, but maintaining these spaces requires different kinds of engagements between residents and urban institutions, and these processes of engagement always evolve (Simone, 2019: 72).

Despite the limited capacity of city governments in Southeast Asia to manage urban development, the ideal image of a city management able to develop sufficient infrastructure and plan for future development remains dominant in Southeast Asia (Bunnell & Goh, 2012). Along with the historical misalignment of planning and realities, the state in Southeast Asia is often distanced from, with limited control over, the society it governs (Kusno, 2019). The result has been often repeated efforts to plan the city that presume a high degree of control over large projects but subsequent failure to uphold regulations (Yap, 2019). Some projects only took place when they gained enough traction through coalition-building among government actors, developers, and possibly civil society leaders. Large projects at strategic areas in the city often involve displacement of existing settlements and communities, even when they maintain the historical fabric of the city (Roberts, 2019). With the idealization of large-scale projects and the appearance of ground-up settlements as "unplanned," planners frame such displacement as for the public good, which is one of the most common reasons for forced evictions around the globe.

Historical perspectives on urban development in Southeast Asia contextualize contemporary development trajectories in a longer timeline. Neglecting the importance of history means ignoring the various layers of urban society and their spatial existence, which might in turn reproduce challenging social issues and uphold problematic constellations of power in urban development. A historical perspective also debunks the government-propounded myth of an idealized planned city unaffected by how urban settlements in Southeast Asia have grown over time. The objective of discussing historical trajectories is not only to gain knowledge about the past but, more importantly, to increase understanding of how urban development in Southeast Asia has led to current trends. The social and political structures of urban societies in Southeast Asia, in general, have relied on self-management of small communities, and the role of the state in governing cities and their local communities has historically been distant in reality (Kusno, 2019). These circumstances do not mean cities in Southeast Asia are inferior to their "planned" counterparts in other regions; rather, cities in Southeast Asia would benefit from moving away from a fixation on top-down master plans and big projects.

3 Planning for Urban Development

In arguing for the importance of learning from history, the previous section started to paint a picture of urban development challenges in Southeast Asia. Terry McGee's term *desakota*, the concept of peri-urbanization, and subsequent terms such as "messy urbanism" (Chalana & Hou, 2016) and "incremental urbanism" (Dovey, 2014) indicate a sense of being in between what is planned and what is organic. Abidin Kusno's "semi-urbanism" (2019) reminds us that this interaction between formal and informal occurs not only along the fringes but also in the city. Furthermore, Kusno (2019: 75) argues that "irregular settlements are constitutive parts of urban development," both in the city and in peri-urban areas. Such patterns emerged at the time new modes of capitalist production kicked in and spurred large-scale industrialization and, eventually, rapid urban transformation in Southeast Asia (Rimmer & Dick, 2009; Jones & Douglass, 2008).

This section shifts the discussion closer to the present day to review the implementation of urban master plans in order to critically scrutinize the "lack of planning" stereotype in Southeast Asia's context. Notwithstanding the uniqueness of the region's urban patterns, sprung from long-term urban development trajectories, many cities remain fixated on the need to have a centralized master plan that relies on regulated control of land. Except Singapore, cities in Southeast Asia struggle to achieve such a goal, yet Singapore's urban planning has become a model to which many city governments aspire. This contradiction has led to a range of challenges, including problems resulting from inconsistent plans.

3.1 Elusive Master Plans

Most cities in Southeast Asia have master plans, but fast-paced changes in cities and problems in getting reliable data on the situation on the ground challenge planners. Moreover, master plans fail to capture the close interaction between the "formal" and "informal" in urban spaces, both in the built environment and in social settings. Two examples, Singapore and Jakarta, illustrate these challenges in Southeast Asia's urban planning.

3.1.1 Singapore: A Model City?

Singapore features two types of formal city plans: concept plans and master plans. The concept plan is a long-term, 40-to-50-year strategic land use and transportation plan, which is reviewed every ten years. Since independence, Singapore has had four concept plans, in 1971, 1991, 2001, and 2011 (URA, 2020a).

The evolution of priorities in concept plans reflects Singapore's gradually increasing involvement in the global economy. In 1971, the focus was fulfilment of basic infrastructure, with housing and transportation as the highest priorities, together with development of new industries as the economy restructured from largely agrarian to industrial. The plan located new housing estates further from the city center, connected by mass transportation, with a nature reserve in the middle. The south of the city, in proximity to the colonial trading port, became the central business district for global finance and the headquarters of corporations, representing Singapore's intention to be the hub of global trade in an industrializing Southeast Asia.

The second concept plan in 1991 placed more emphasis on business parks, academic institutions, scientific research, and high-tech industries, aligning with the expanding knowledge economy of the region (Forbes, 2019). Southeast Asia was shifting from flows of goods from manufacturing industries to flows of human capital. Developing a formal education and research agenda became part of an urban strategy, as cities participate in the globalizing knowledge economy. Projects to expand formal education institutions to attract international students, however, mostly came after the turn of the millennium.

The Singapore Concept Plan 2001 boasted of cultivating "a thriving world-class city in the 21st century, with rich heritage, character, diversity and identity" (URA, 2020c). A distinctive feature of the Concept Plan 2001 was the "Identity Plan," represented by fifteen nodes, each with a special character that becomes a theme of their built environment, and a "Parks and Waterbodies Plan" to present an array of recreational areas. These foci sustained attention on attracting human capital, particularly urban managers, whom planners touted as the "creative class" (Florida, 2005). However, an urban strategy of catering to the "creative class" has received criticism around the world for its tendency to induce gentrification and thus to increase the costs of urban services and housing. Such concerns also emerged in Singapore in the first decade of the new millennium. The rapid increase in property prices was also driven by a change in public housing provision, from a supply-driven to a demand-driven mode, and the pegging of public housing prices to private housing prices. Concern over housing prices led to one of the focus areas under Concept Plan 2011, in which "good affordable homes with a full range of amenities" was a strategy "to sustain a high-quality living environment" (URA, 2020d).

The shifting priorities in every concept plan are indicative of the rapid evolution of the city. Recognizing the pace of change, a master plan guides urban development for a shorter stretch of ten to fifteen years and, based on a requirement in the Planning Act 1959, is reviewed every five years (URA, 2020b). The Singapore Improvement Trust (SIT) formulated the first master plan in the mid-1950s, prior to introduction of the strategic long-term concept plan system. The master plan, now under the Urban Redevelopment Authority (URA), includes more detailed land use plans for every planning area in Singapore (Singapore Government, 2019; Lee, 2015). The current master plan designates five planning areas in Singapore – West, North, Central, North-East, and East – with zoning and plot ratios[1] for each. Before the Minister of National Development approves it, the master plan must be gazetted for "a period of not less than two weeks within which the public may make objections and representations concerning it" (Lee, 2015: 7).

City governments elsewhere in Southeast Asia have often hailed Singapore's urban planning as a model to follow. Priorities and focus areas might shift, and details have been amended after regular reviews, but urban development has seemed to consistently follow the concept plans and master plans. However, even a city as formally planned as Singapore has seen cases in which changes preceded the master plan review. A case in point was the development of a new road that removed part of an old cemetery, Bukit Brown. The road plan was announced by the government in 2011, although it was not in the master plan yet at the time of its announcement. The road's delineation only appeared in the Draft Master Plan 2013 (Lee, 2015). The subject of natural and heritage conservation became a matter for debate when Master Plan 2013 was revealed for public feedback, drawing questions from the Singapore Heritage Society and the Nature Society. This case shows that, although urban development in Singapore was relatively consistent with what has been planned, there was still a possibility of initiating a development project outside the plan, preceding the next master plan – and also the possibility of public resistance to the state's schemes.

3.1.2 Jakarta: Master Plan

Jakarta is a case in which the gaps between formal urban plans and reality are significant. The city government has constantly updated master plans, but implementation has been inconsistent. Thus far, updates have been more about reflecting changes that have occurred than directing future developments. Observers have pointed to the influence of private investors and developers in driving urban development as one reason for inconsistencies in plan implementation. Their influence is often strong enough to push through projects that do not meet the directions of the master plan (Salim et al., 2018).

---

[1] A plot ratio is the maximum gross floor area of a building development compared to the land on which it sits.

Like Singapore's first concept plan in 1971, Jakarta's first master plan in 1965 – named *Rencana Induk Jakarta* – was a comprehensive urban plan with emphases on public transportation, green zones, environmental issues, and the regional impact of Jakarta's development as the capital city. Train and underground subway systems were main parts of the public transportation plan to support Jakarta's population, projected to reach 6.5 million by 1985. Eventually, Jakarta's population in 1985 reached approximately 7 million, not far from the projection, but the subway system did not get built and was only launched in 2019 when the population had already passed 10 million. Instead of achieving the planned greenbelt around the city and the flood mitigation strategies the plan proposed, green areas in Jakarta were converted into large development projects over time (Rukmana, 2015), reflecting the strong political and economic roles of large developers in influencing and changing the formal master plan.

The updated *Rencana Umum Tata Ruang Jakarta* (Spatial Plan) 1985–2005 no longer featured trains as a public transportation solution but had dedicated bus lanes with double-decker buses. The dedicated bus lanes were only built in 2003 and did not include double-decker buses. By then, significant developments already did not adhere to the spatial plan. Some of these inconsistencies were imposed by the national government during Suharto's presidency (1966–98), which centralized many resources and development initiatives in Jakarta. Decrees from the national government often overruled the spatial plan. For example, the northwest coast of Jakarta, which the spatial plan allocated as part of a coastal forest to prevent land subsidence, became prime real estate for a consortium of private developers that obtained the permit by national government decree. Another presidential decree in 1995 allowed large private developers to reclaim 10,000 hectares of land in Jakarta Bay, converting the northern green belt into residential and commercial zones. Eventually the conversion of green areas in Jakarta Bay became a formal feature in the next spatial plan, *Rencana Tata Ruang Wilayah Jakarta* 2000–10. This plan featured reclamation of artificial islands off the coast of Jakarta Bay, as well as a new flood mitigation strategy that relied on a large sea wall.

From 1985 to 2005, there were at least thirty violations of Jakarta's master plan by large developments (Rukmana, 2015). Such violations were typically conversions of areas that were originally designated to be water catchments, protected forests, urban forests, and general green areas, adding up to 9,701 acres of land. All these violations were eventually included in the subsequent master plan, *Rencana Tata Ruang Wilayah* 2010, as existing land use.

More recently, private developers have been able to negotiate official plot ratios by paying "compensation funds" for exceeding the floor-to-area ratio in the master plan. Jakarta's government has used these funds to build public infrastructure, such as roads and public housing, without going through the official city budget. Some of the new public infrastructure built with these "compensation funds" has not been in the existing master plan. A well-known case was the *Simpang Susun Semanggi*, a circular flyover at a cloverleaf junction in the central business district. Construction of the flyover started in 2016, with funds from Mitra Panca Persada, a subsidiary of Mori Building Company from Japan. The flyover was financed by compensation funds the company paid for breaching the plot ratio on a new building project. The flyover itself was not in the master plan, but it became a popular development project, as the Jakarta government publicly promoted it as an effort to alleviate the city's worsening traffic jams. The same mechanism came into play when Muara Wisesa Samudra, a subsidiary company of a larger developer, Agung Podomoro Land, paid for the Muara Angke housing flats development with compensation funds to pave the way for developing an offshore reclamation islet (Siswanto & Raharjo, 2016).

Instead of using their authority to uphold the city's master plan, the city government and the national government have played roles in violating it. The government has authorized violations of the master plan through both formal and informal negotiations, and it has framed mechanisms like "compensation funds" publicly as innovative steps rather than violations. Inconsistencies in the master plan's implementation and negotiations to change land use and density allocations have revealed government institutions' weakness in upholding regulations and the influence of "elite informal networks" involving "real estate, national political parties and the military" in gearing urban development toward profit-making speculation (Herlambang et al., 2019: 645). Such practices have been reminiscent of Ananya Roy's (2009: 84) conceptualization of the state as "an informalized entity," with reference to planning in India, although the issue in Jakarta was less the inability to plan than the process of continuous and contradictory adjustments. Many changes to facilitate profit-making interests in urban development have been eventually legalized through official alterations of the master plan or through executive interventions.

Rather than indicating a lack of planning, inconsistencies in master plan implementation in Jakarta have represented a disconnect between assumptions of what planning is supposed to do and the realities of urban politics, both politics among elites and everyday politics on the ground. Although big developers are dominant actors, there have been occasions when civil society groups manage to push through their demands. Such dynamics have been most observable in terms of the role of human agency in neighborhoods to negotiate, to resist, or to take part in the urban transformation of Southeast Asia. We will return to that agency in Section 4, on urban social movements, and in Section 6, on Southeast Asia's urban futures. The misalignments and mismatches between formal urban development plans and their implementation, such as those we see in Jakarta, have demonstrated the necessity for studies of urban development to connect formal processes with realities on the ground, beyond master plan documents that might or might not be consistent with actual practice.

3.2 Planning versus Informality?

The most obvious example to underscore the importance of understanding cities differently concerns the ways in which scholars of urban development have discussed "informality." While it has often been understood as the opposite of formal social systems, informality in the context of Southeast Asia's urban development has been inseparable from the formal. In urban development, informality regularly refers to economic activities and settlements. Economic activities that are categorized as "informal" engage 60 percent of the workforce in the Asia-Pacific region (ILO, 2019). On the one hand, this formal/informal differentiation has reinforced the need for technocratic planning, with a sense of the formal's superiority. On the other hand, challenging such a dichotomy raises the risk of falling into exoticization and romanticization of the social fabric of the "informal" in attempts to advocate for appreciation, if the discussion lacks deep understanding of the complexities involved. In reality, all economic actors function in relation to each other and blur such boundaries. Informal economies may obtain legal status through advocacy and lobbying of local governments (Matejowsky & Milgram, 2019), for instance, while governments and officials might establish relationships with nonstate groups to maintain stability and order at the grassroots level. For example, Ian Wilson's work (2011) on protection regimes in post-1998 Jakarta found groups that range from local urban thugs to religious leaders that function as "middle regimes," working in coordination with government actors to control small businesses, including informal businesses on the streets and in settlements. Such an ecosystem of political and economic actors might, in extreme cases, allow for extrajudicial actions. But many do not go to such extreme and have become part of everyday life, such as in the spatial organization of street vendors in many cities.

In urban planning and popular discourses, "unplanned," "informal" areas in the city often refer to self-built settlements, neither planned by city officials nor sanctioned by regulations. The term "informal," therefore, indicates an inferior quality of structures and infrastructures. Such assumptions ignore the fact that inferior parts of the built environment, if any, result from growing social inequality and power imbalances in urban development. Governments have not formally recognized many settlements that have existed since the colonial period because of their lack of access to legal means to seek recognition, and some residents might not consider "formalization" important because they have inherited the land across generations (Kusno, 2019). In cities in Indonesia, for example, the lack of affordable housing spurred densification of these settlements as economic centralization took place. Such urban development combined with the colonial-era legacy of Indigenous compounds' operating relatively autonomously in the city in deciding who could settle in them (Perkasa, Padawangi & Farida, 2021).

Closer examination reveals the formal and informal to be more interdependent than dichotomous. Like peasants in rural areas who might not have land titles, urban dwellers might also lack land titles, because land titling processes in many cities in Southeast Asia are incomplete. However, both long-term residents and new urban dwellers in areas without land titles might provide affordable housing and services in the absence of sufficient government programs. Lack of government regulations or programs, or failure to implement state programs, gives the impression that these grassroots initiatives are unplanned. Nevertheless, in-depth studies in these areas have shown the existence of some kind of order, with "intricate arrangements and mobilities across different sectors of organization, different logics of authority and work ... [and] a plurality of engagement between residents and different urban institutions" (Simone, 2019: 72), even though these programs are not government-controlled. Indeed, residents take pains "to support the necessary myths of given authorities – to sustain the impression of an overarching order" (Simone, 2019: 72).

Because the term "informal" is value-laden, as lacking formal regulations and order, some urban studies scholars of Southeast Asia have used alternative terms. For example, AbdouMaliq Simone (2014) uses "relational," as in a "relational economy" that relies on actions and reactions, social reciprocity, and the flexibility to plan for different scenarios and possible outcomes. Abidin Kusno (2019) uses the terms "semi-urbanism" and, later on, "middling urbanism" to convey the mix of "official" and "nonofficial" in the city. Taking the example of the *kampung* settlement in Jakarta to illustrate semi-urbanism, Kusno (2019: 77–78) writes: "The land on which the building[s] stand ... may lack legal status, but this does not mean that the settlement is illegal ... The characteristic of the *kampung* is such that its domain can be considered as different from the formally planned parts of Jakarta yet is also tied to 'all systems of domination,' both confirming and deconstructing power."

The relative autonomy of small enclaves in the city to craft, change, and build their places, socially and physically, illustrates the possibilities of grassroots initiatives. Crafted from the bottom up, spaces from the grassroots are results of negotiations and efforts by various actors who consistently prepare for multiple possible scenarios, embodying a different process than found in top-down technocratic approaches (Simone, 2014). These bottom-up initiatives might result in fragmented and pragmatic responses to policies and projects, but at some moments of political opportunity they might create small civic spaces – the spaces in which discussions, debates, and negotiations take place – for concerted transformative change.

3.3 Planning and "Leveling"

Cities in Southeast Asia are agglomerations of these small enclaves of places that may be relatively autonomous and heterogeneous in their development, but the money economy, standardization of processes, public facilities, and cultural institutions may exert some "leveling" influence, albeit "adjusted to mass requirements" (Wirth, 1938: 18). This influence is more applicable in the context of authoritative city governments that are capable of standardizing public services and imposing commonly acceptable cultural practices. An example is Singapore, where the government has standardized educational institutions, public services, and planning processes and has identified certain topics such as race and religion as sensitive issues that require special care in public discussions, including for the design and use of urban space. However, this is not the case in most cities in the region. Just as master plans end in patchy implementation in other cities, the "leveling" influence of overarching institutions and norms on the city has been continuously negotiated.

With the increasing scale of cities' heterogeneity, population, and spatial expansion has come fragmentation among different groups about what the city should be. Policymakers' persistent aspirations to exercise a "leveling" influence over a range of different grassroots-level aspirations, however, have resulted in their claiming that the city offers what the mass of the population requires. These claims might be despite a significant gap between benefits for one group and losses for others. For example, across cities in Southeast Asia, old residences have been cleared for big developments and ordinary settlements demolished to make way for infrastructure projects in the name of making the city better. Many of these changes have forcefully affected the urban poor (Padawangi, 2019). Also, new modes of motorized transportation affect how planners design urban spaces and mobility, as they phase out old modes of transportation in the name of modernization, along with those workers (Figure 4). Authorities often present those development projects as facilitating public goods such as flood protection, recreational spaces, and transportation

Figure 4 *Becak* – a traditional form of three-wheel-cycle transportation that was widely used in the early years of Jakarta's post-independence urban development – has become marginalized as the contemporary city prioritizes motorized transport in its planning. City government had previously outlawed *becak* as it was considered a hindrance to traffic, although since 2018 it has been legal again as a result of advocacy and lobbying by urban poor activists and the *becak* peddler union in Jakarta.

Source: Author, 2019.

efficiency, but in a heterogeneous, fragmented, and unequal society the projects entail marginalization.

Urban development has become a process of marginalization of those who are less politically and economically powerful. Large-scale development projects and "urban boosterism" – that is, projects aimed at "projecting a positive image of a city . . . to attract investors, professionals and white-collar workers" (Kong, 2007: 386) – compete with settlement enclaves for space and resources to influence the culture of the city and the identity of city dwellers. Many of these projects have been imposed by higher levels of government, such as provincial or national governments, or by a dominant private-sector player in the economy. Amidst this unbalanced spatial competition, obtaining in-depth knowledge of everyday lived realities through a grounded perspective has become increasingly important for planners and scholars. There is a pressing need to refocus urban development to address ongoing injustices and to bring human agency and political life – space for discussion and debate to inform decision-making, rather than top-down technocratic approaches – into the making of cities.

4 Studying Urban Development in Southeast Asia

The tandem between technocratic planning and global capitalism may seem to dominate the political spaces of urban development in the region, but the domination has been, and continues to be, incomplete. Massive modernization projects – encompassing local, national, and transnational financial powers that compete as well as collude in urban development – have effected large-scale transformations of urban landscapes, but they have met with grassroots initiatives that range from pragmatic compliance to resistance, with strategies ranging from mundane everyday practices to organized social movements. In Indonesia and the Philippines, for example, collective actions within civil society against forced evictions and for the rights of the urban poor are visible and relatively well-organized. In Thailand, advocacy for housing rights has led to a nationwide participatory housing program for the poor (Archer, 2019). Foiled by such pushback, most states of Southeast Asia have not been fully effective in implementing technocratic visions of urban development.

The spectrum of grassroots initiatives around urban development in Southeast Asia can only be understood through a careful examination of local social practices. Under pressures of neoliberal developmentalism and a spectrum of political authoritarianism that stifles political spaces, small and localized city enclaves still operate their social mechanisms. These local spaces are hard to see on the surface, yet they are prevalent in everyday urban life. These local spaces are easily dismissed, or even misunderstood, since their mechanisms are difficult to understand for those who are not part of them. Nevertheless, exploring them is important for gaining a critical perspective on urban development. Studies from cities in Southeast Asia have uncovered some of these local practices and have suggested a different understanding of urban development in parallel with the presumptive all-encompassing neoliberal capitalism.

The attention to these small enclaves of grassroots' efforts represents a conscious effort to develop a critical understanding of urban development as political. Groundedness does not mean that all studies of urban development must be on a micro scale; rather, it is a necessary perspective to allow one to scale up spatially from the smallest neighborhoods to cities and then to metropolitan, national, and global levels without losing sight of actual lived experiences. Without deep knowledge of and connections with communities, research projects might deploy methods that perpetuate power imbalances in urban development. A straightforward example is when a research project describes a lack of infrastructure in one neighborhood in a central area of the city. Inability to go deeper to understand historical, political, and social constraints and the extent to which the cultural life of the communities in question relates to the larger urban context would risk the study's justifying removal of these communities to make way for top-down or scaled-up projects with perceivably "better" infrastructure (Padawangi, 2019). In this case, a research project becomes a tool that paints destruction as utilitarian – for the good of the majority – but this is problematic if the researcher's limited understanding of the communities involved obscures unequal power structures. Such patterns fit the frames of neoliberal governance and global capitalism that continue to destroy social fabric at the local level.

4.1 Limitations of Official Datasets

What tools do we have at hand to study urban development without perpetuating unequal power structures – but still with capacity to affect policymaking? The familiar ways in which authorities have collected and framed urban-development-related data that feed into policymaking complicate such efforts. For example, the United Nations issues its World Urbanization Prospects annually, but these aggregate data are problematic because the definition and measurement of the "urban" may vary from one country to another. Hence, the conclusions they suggest may be misleading (Jones, 2019).

Studying urban development for comparative perspective in Southeast Asia also raises the issue of city size categorization. Globally, the term "megacity" refers to a city with a population of more than 10 million. Currently in Southeast Asia there are only a few megacities. Metro Manila is an agglomeration of seventeen cities that accounts for 12.7 percent of the Philippines' population, while Jakarta, which accounts for 7.1 percent of Indonesia's population, comprises part of the mega-urban region Jabodetabek (an acronym for Jakarta, Bogor, Depok, Tangerang, and Bekasi) that accounts for 11 percent of the total population of the country. In Southeast Asia, except for Singapore as a city-state, each country has one or two cities with significant shares of the population. Phnom Penh is home to 51.4 percent of the population of Cambodia; Bangkok comprises 14.7 percent of the population of Thailand; Hanoi and Ho Chi Minh City together account for almost 13 percent of the population of Vietnam; Vientiane contains about 12 percent of the population of Laos; and Yangon contains almost 10 percent of the population of Myanmar (UN, 2018).

Therefore, the 10 million population cut-off is not very useful in understanding urban development in the region (Jones, 2019).

Rather than taking a particular number of residents as a threshold to categorize a megacity, one may look at the impact of a city's social and economic dominance for the country's population. Such dominance is often referred to as characterizing a "primate city" (Rimmer & Dick, 2009). In any case, analysis based on population numbers must take into account what insight those numbers give into the social, cultural, economic, and political life of the city (see Table 1).

Therefore, in conducting comparative studies, researchers need to consider at least three aspects: 1) that the comparison is specific to a certain period of time, since issues related to urban development in the region may change over time; 2) that the purpose of comparison is clear, with the case studies chosen for a specific purpose, and that the researchers remain mindful of possibilities and problems of generalizing from their findings; and 3) that the comparison be attuned to inequalities in experience of urbanization among different stakeholders (Koh, 2019). Comparable case studies may not align neatly with official population-based categories, nor may they compare all aspects of urbanization. For example, the World Bank's agglomeration index, which measures density of urban economic activity and settlement, does not capture the unequal economic opportunities among different urban populations, though the index is still useful to identify the development of concentrated urban corridors (Jones, 2019).

The issues with officially reported data do not mean these data are not usable. There are at least two methods to address accuracy issues among quantitative datasets across different cities and countries in the region. First, it is important to be grounded – to have a good grasp of lived/grassroots realities in urban areas – before assessing datasets from official sources. Corroborating trends obtained from large datasets with field observations is the best way to learn about the limitations of datasets, in order to be able to interpret findings in light of these limitations. For example, residency data from a civil registry might not capture unregistered migrants who find housing through informal channels. Income and employment data might not capture those who work in the informal economy, so treating the data as if they represent the population might be misleading. In the case of Myanmar, for instance, quantitative data have been limited, and long-term trends were almost impossible to analyze through census data because most surveys before 2014 were partial (Roberts, 2019). To gain knowledge of realities on the ground, an in-depth qualitative approach is the most useful.

Second, new technologies can be helpful to make sense of the continuously transforming boundaries of cities, including through peri-urbanization and

Table 1 List of megacities and primate cities of Southeast Asia

Country/area	City	Statistical concept	City population (thousands)			Average annual rate of change (%)		City population as percentage of country/area population (2018)	City population as percentage of urban population in the country/area (2018)
			2000	2018	2030	2000–18	2018–30		
Cambodia	Phnom Penh*	Urban agglomeration	1,149	1,952	2,805	2.9	3.0	12.0	51.4
Indonesia	Jakarta**	Metropolitan area	8,390	10,517	12,687	1.3	1.6	3.9	7.1
	Surabaya	City proper	2,611	2,903	3,413	0.6	1.4	1.1	2.0
Lao PDR	Vientiane*	City proper		828^		1.6		12.0^^	31.0^^
Malaysia	Kuala Lumpur*	Metropolitan area	4,176	7,564	9,805	3.3	2.2	23.6	31.0
Myanmar	Mandalay	Urban agglomeration	847	1,374	1,757	2.7	2.1	2.6	8.3
	Yangon*	Urban agglomeration	3,573	5,157	6,389	2.0	1.8	9.6	31.3

Philippines	Davao	City proper	1,152	1,745	2,256	2.3	2.1	1.6	3.5
	Metro Manila**	Metropolitan area	9,958	13,482	16,841	1.7	1.9	12.7	27.0
Singapore	Singapore	Urban agglomeration	3,914	5,792	6,342	2.2	0.8	100	100
Thailand	Chiang Mai	Urban agglomeration	407	1,135	1,318	5.7	1.2	1.6	3.3
	Krung Thep (Bangkok)**	Urban agglomeration	6,395	10,156	12,101	2.6	1.5	14.7	29.4
Vietnam	Ha Noi	Urban agglomeration	1,660	4,283	6,362	5.3	3.3	4.4	12.4
	Ho Chi Minh City**	Urban agglomeration	4,389	8,145	11,054	3.4	2.5	8.4	23.5

** Megacity and primate city

* Primate city

^ http://unstats.un.org/unsd/demographic/products/dyb/dyb2.htm

^^ http://data.un.org/CountryProfile.aspx

Note: Not all countries in Southeast Asia are represented. Timor-Leste and Brunei Darussalam are notably missing from this table.

Source: UN, 2018.

urban agglomeration. Gavin Jones (2019) pointed to the "surrounding areas" of cities as one factor that complicates the study of Southeast Asia's urban development, especially around the megacities. The "messy" surroundings of a city exemplify populations and economies that are linked to the urban, but population categories in aggregated datasets usually strictly follow the city's administrative boundaries. This "messiness" reflects gray areas where city authorities' functional control diminishes but urban political and economic processes continue. Such gray areas manifest governments' incomplete control, as discussed previously in Section 3, and are important areas to study, but data categorizations and existing definitions are insufficient to fully understand the dynamics of urban development in Southeast Asia (Jones, 2019; Cairns, 2019). The situation gets more complicated when urban agglomerations form mega-urban regions (MURs), spurring more urban development projects with rising pressure to convert agricultural land and labor into nonagricultural to increase "economic productivity" (Jones & Douglass, 2008).

Remote sensing data from satellite and airborne imaging technologies can provide bases for comparison across the region (Jones, 2019). Stephen Cairns (2019) has argued that remotely sensed data can also assist in alleviating "city-centricity" in studying urbanization, because urban development affects not only cities but also rural areas and rural–urban hybrid landscapes. He explains: "In Southeast Asia, where empirical data is so often patchy, poorly managed or even absent, remotely sensed data is an indispensable resource for understanding demographics, city footprints and urban extents" (Cairns, 2019: 123). These remotely sensed data still need cleaning up, though, because of conditions that may affect data accuracy, such as light pollution, clouds, and other kinds of "noise" (Vollmer et al., 2015). One way to complement and clean remotely sensed data is by checking the details for selected sites through field-based ethnography. Another approach that is increasingly popular to supplement large datasets is data crowdsourcing through open-source mapping platforms (Padawangi et al., 2016).

4.2 Deciphering "Messiness" from Below

An important vantage point in studying cities from Southeast Asia, therefore, is one that looks beyond official categories to decipher urban realities. Rather than judging these cities as "messy" or "poorly planned," the researcher can perceive the "unknown" of urban processes that require further attention. The two approaches to address accuracy issues just discussed – cross-checking official data with qualitative field research or data from new technologies – reflect different scales of understanding: while one scales upward to remote sensing, the other scales down to micro-level corroboration. Both require different skillsets, but they complement each other. However, the micro-level grounded perspective may be at odds with the task of identifying general trends that policymaking requires. Therefore, groundedness should be consistent with efforts to obtain a larger picture rather than offering only a fragmented understanding of Southeast Asia's urban life. Attention to everyday lived realities should not neglect understanding of the larger context but should connect across scales.

An important feature of groundedness, and how this micro-level approach allows a big-picture perspective, is the consciousness it facilitates of power inequalities in urban development, both in outcomes and in processes. Those processes include the research that goes into policymaking, including research that intends to address injustices. Hence, a micro-scale perspective on everyday lived realities may emphasize bringing human agency, especially that of the marginalized groups, into urban development politics. Those less powerful groups are more likely to be in the "messy" category of urban spaces and are more likely to experience top-down interventions to make up for a perceived "lack of planning." Closer examination of common categories of marginalized groups in the city, which intersect with sociological categories of economic class, gender, and race, reveals how groundedness can lend nuance to otherwise limited top-down perspectives.

4.2.1 The Urban Poor

The urban poor in general are marginalized in the context of capitalist urban development. In Southeast Asia, like in other parts of the world, urban poverty levels – the percentage of the population in poverty – are generally lower than rural poverty levels. However, the poverty level is usually calculated based on a certain threshold for income and basic needs fulfilment. While useful in describing the magnitude of poverty to a certain extent, poverty levels become problematic when compared across cities and countries because of differences in how they are calculated (see Table 2). They may not reflect other possibilities and opportunities for grassroots advocacy as well as social capital among communities to help their members escape poverty. In other words, the poverty level does not indicate aspects of empowerment of the urban poor that may allow more long-term efforts for sustainable poverty alleviation.

Studying the urban poor from below requires looking beyond distribution of wealth and resources to develop a grounded understanding of their roles – both existing and potential – in urban politics. The interaction among the urban poor, activists, policymakers, and political candidates opens possibilities for the

Table 2 Urban Poverty in Southeast Asia

Country	Year	Level of urban poverty (%)
Brunei Darussalam	n.a.	n.a.
Cambodia	2012	6.4
Indonesia	2014	8.3
Lao People's Democratic Republic	2012	10.0
Malaysia	2014	0.3**
Myanmar	2017	11.3*
Philippines	2012	13.0
Singapore	2017	7***
Thailand	2013	7.7
Timor-Leste	2007	45.2
Vietnam	2014	3.8

*   World Bank, 2017

**   EPU, 2012

*** Based on Singapore Statistics data on households with income below $1,000 per month, living in one-room subsidized rental flats. Singapore does not have an official poverty line. The data do not include low-income migrant workers on work passes, such as construction workers in dormitories and domestic workers, who comprise approximately 20 percent of the population.

Source: UN-Habitat World Cities Report 2016.

urban poor to influence urban development. This interaction varies across the region, with some cities being more open to urban poor advocacy and influence than others. It is important to realize that the urban poor are not just the recipients of subsidies, burdens to the budget, or vote banks that they are often stereotyped as being. The urban poor are a political force in urban development who require further study because their roles are more nuanced than development policies have portrayed.

The political role of the urban poor starts from these communities' comparable situations in urban development across various cities. First, individuals in this income group usually struggle to secure spaces in the city. Not all of them are migrants, but lack of affordable housing options limits choices for migrants who settle in the city, as discussed in Section 3.2 on planning and informality. Residents of older urban neighborhoods may also face displacement because of gentrification, a process by which wealthier newcomers, with different lifestyle requirements, replace another group within the population. In addition, many of the urban poor population face difficulties in securing tenure for their land because they lack access to legal aid, combined with incomplete and problematic land registration systems throughout most of Southeast Asia. In some cases, discriminatory practices in land registration among certain ethnic groups and corrupt practices in providing land registration services have also limited access to secure land tenure for the poor. This insecurity results in precarious situations for the urban poor, as rapid spatial transformations continue to cater to the role of cities as political and economic centers.

Second, many of the urban poor face challenges in acquiring urban services. Table 3 provides a snapshot of how much of the urban population lack access to services in Southeast Asia. These numbers are unlikely to be precise, given the difficulty of capturing exact quantitative information for those in informal settings. Nevertheless, they indicate that the issue of access to urban services and infrastructure extends to a considerable share of the population. Residents in areas lacking in infrastructure must find other ways to meet basic needs. When individuals cannot depend on the government, they may rely on other powerful groups that provide such services at higher cost. For example, city water providers often deny the poor water services. In such situations, the poor need to get their water from sellers who charge them much more than the water utility company charges the middle- and upper-class customers it serves (Padawangi & Vallée, 2016). Informal racketeering regimes may also exist

Table 3 Proportion of urban population with insufficient improved water, sanitation, durable housing, and living area in countries of Southeast Asia, 2014

Country	Proportion of urban population with insufficient improved water, sanitation, durable housing, and living area (%)
Brunei Darussalam	n.a.
Cambodia	55.1%
Indonesia	21.8%
Lao People's Democratic Republic	31.4%
Malaysia	n.a.
Myanmar	41.0%
Philippines	38.3%
Singapore	n.a.
Thailand	25%
Timor-Leste	n.a.
Vietnam	27.2%

Source: UN-Habitat, 2015.

under the protection of government actors, adding more expenses and layers of control (Wilson, 2011).

Attention toward the urban poor as a political force is important to give more nuance to analyses of urban politics. The case of Jakarta's gubernatorial election in 2017, in which a challenger who developed friendly relations with conservative religious groups defeated an incumbent candidate from a minority ethnic group and religion, illustrates this point. While many observers at the time claimed the process and result were largely about religion and discrimination, a closer analysis that considers the political role of the urban poor demonstrates the significance also of urban development policies for votes – particularly forced evictions of the poor and development concessions the incumbent granted mostly to Chinese-Indonesian elite developers (Savirani & Aspinall, 2017; Gani, 2018). This case shows how class consciousness intersects with religious and ethnic identity in urban politics, as well as how urban development projects embody that intersection.

Local and regional advocacy groups and networks of urban poor have emerged across Southeast Asia. To different degrees, the urban poor in various countries in the region have organized and attempted to address common issues they face. Representatives from Indonesia, Cambodia, Myanmar, the Philippines, Thailand, and Vietnam joined, too, in formalizing a regionwide network with the Declaration of Commitment and Action of the Urban Poor Coalition Asia. Its commitments include developing a savings and financial system to support community-based housing efforts, community-based mapping, securing land for housing, and capacity building, as well as citywide networked collaborations, including with local authorities and agencies (UPCA, 2012). The establishment of the UPCA is linked with the work of the Asian Coalition for Housing Rights (ACHR), particularly its program on the Asian Coalition for Community Action (ACCA), to which we return in this Element's final section on urban futures.

4.2.2 Gendered Spaces

The politics of urban development require scrutiny into women's representation in policymaking and the resulting built environment, as gender inequality is also part of power inequality. Urban inequality is in not just economic but also social and cultural power, including in "gendered and racialized spaces" (Sarkar & De, 2002: 6). As a region of "uneven capitalist development combined with enormous local diversity," Southeast Asia and its urbanizing landscape show "processes of state and nation formation, global economic restructuring, and overseas labor migration" that have "created fluid geographies of gender, race, and class that cut across national boundaries" (Ong & Peletz, 1995: 8). Besides the creation of gendered industries, with more women working in the growing garment and textile industries under the "new international division of labor" that developed with economic globalization starting around the 1970s, the social and economic transformations urbanization causes bring different experiences of urban spaces along gender lines. Urban spaces are sites of "political agency and contested power," places in which the material and symbolic are important in their gendering and "sexing" (Tonkiss, 2005).

The growing number of women being absorbed into the industrialized work-force and gaining access to public services such as education and healthcare represent an important impact of urban development for women. However, gender inequalities in Southeast Asia's urbanization recommend in-depth quali-tative corroboration of these numbers. Representations of gendered bodies are separable neither from local cultural and nationalist discourses nor from mater-ial realities of urban development. "Postcolonial forces of dislocation, ethnic heterogeneity, nation-building, and international business have blurred, con-fused, and made problematic cultural understandings of what it means to be male or female in local societies" (Ong & Peletz, 1995: 4). On the one hand, the association of women with nurturing and domestic roles – "refined and modest, dependent and subordinate wife or daughter" (Hatley, 2002: 132) – in combin-ation with urbanizing landscapes had propelled women to find particular eco-nomic opportunities. For example, women in rural Thailand, especially in the 1990s, ventured into becoming food sellers as "relatively autonomous business-people," although still without the status of white-collar women in the capitalist economy (Yasmeen, 2002). On the other hand, the stereotype of "docile and obedient" women, derived from this idealized construction, also led rural women to be perceived as suitable workers in manufacturing industries under male superiors (Warouw, 2019). Yet, as the industrialization of Southeast Asia brought/incurred feminization of the labor force, labor activism increased/ thrived in urban industrial centers, even under authoritarian regimes such as that in Indonesia under Suharto (1965–98). Women's labor activism grew through a combination of factors, including freedom from traditionally imposed gender constraints, especially for migrant women (Silvey, 2003), and increased connections with nongovernmental organizations (NGOs) (Mills, 2005) and transnational feminist networks (Ford, 2008).

The transformation of gendered spaces in urban development is more com-plicated than just a story of women's empowerment. The growth of women's activism in urban centers of Southeast Asia does not eradicate the assumption of the female as delicate, prone to crime and harassment. Women's appearance in controlled environments, such as shopping malls, is generally considered more acceptable and hence has led to the stereotypical capitalist-consumer-culture association of urban women with shopping. Gendered stereotypes shape one's opportunities in the public sphere but, at the same time, construct specific realms for social activism. For example, it was a protest by women in Indonesia in 1998 that eventually snowballed into the series of demonstrations that led to the resignation of President Suharto. *Suara Ibu Peduli* (The Voices of Concerned Mothers, SIP) staged a protest in February 1998 against rising milk prices amidst the Asian financial crisis. A popular conservative newspaper scorned them as "mothers who did not breastfeed their children," but they continued to bring tools of housewives into public space during their protests, expanding the nurturing image of women beyond the boundaries of the home as "concerned mothers of the nation" (Budianta, 2003). This maternalist ideology inspired SIP women and those who joined them after the first protest, much as happened during the women's suffrage movement in the United States, in the context of which Margaret Dreier Robins from Brooklyn called all women "to mother the world by entering the arena of the larger society through suffrage, politics, and the professions" (Flanagan, 2002: 118).

The persistence of maternalist ideology in urbanizing Southeast Asia has thus far opened women's access to the public sphere but also limited their range. Unlike the suffragettes of the US progressive era, SIP women in Indonesia did not push for professional involvement in society but built their activism around addressing everyday problems, including securing affordable milk, basic food, and children's scholarships, and helping women establish small businesses in their communities (Pujiwati & Upik, 2007). The case of rural Thai women who work as food sellers in Bangkok, for instance, demonstrates this same tension: the stereotype of women as nurturing caregivers and good cooks boosts their business but also limits the women by entrapping them in low-profit jobs. The persistence of idealized gender images also leads to gendered aspirations despite wider education and economic opportunities for women. Ariane Utomo's research on college students in Jakarta and Makassar (2005) found that even many female college students saw domesticity as their main role, as their society expects them to prioritize family upon motherhood.

Urban development also opens opportunities for wider expressions of marginalized gender identities and sexualities, but "heterosexist and classist systems" persist in Southeast Asian cities, as "gendered temporal and spatial symbols" retain the power "to control lived space and material resources" (Sarker & De, 2002: 2–3; see also Jackson, 2001). Lesbian, gay, bisexual, and transgender (LGBT) communities are socially marginalized because their identities and lifestyles are considered taboo. In the Philippines and Thailand, displays of "homoeroticism and transgenderism" are "publicly tolerated but still derided" (Jackson, 2001: 5). Indeed, there are openly transgender or homosexual public figures in the city-centered entertainment industry, such as Dorce Gamalama, a famous Indonesian transgender actress, and Kumar, the first openly gay Singapore entertainer. However, many are forced to live in the shadows of society, and even in highly urbanized Singapore homosexual intercourse between two men is illegal. In Indonesia, the presence of *waria* or *banci* (Indonesian terms for transgender people) is widely known, but they are subjected to marginalization and exoticization in everyday life. Trans brothels in Singapore's Bugis Street were famous among British naval servicemen in the 1960s, but upon the closure of the brothels the trans women faced discrimination when applying for service jobs. Other aspects of discrimination, including "silence and invisibility" surrounding LGBT people in social life (Oetomo, 2001), affect how marginalized gender groups experience and are represented in urban spaces and planning processes.

4.2.3 Migration

Migration is not a recent phenomenon in urban development. Historically, the role of migrants has been not just economic but also social and cultural. Louis Wirth (1938: 2) wrote of the city's attraction/appeal: "The city is not only in ever larger degrees the dwelling-place and the workshop of modern man [and woman], but it is the initiating and controlling center of economic, political and cultural life that has drawn the most remote parts of the world into its orbit and woven diverse areas, peoples, and activities into a cosmos." This characterization applies to all large cities in contemporary Southeast Asia: a good number of their population were not born there. In the largest cities of countries in the region, the birth rate is rather low compared to that elsewhere in the country, but the rate of in-migration may be higher (Table 4). The lowest urban birth rate in Southeast Asia is currently in Singapore, at 1.2 live births per 1,000 population per year, but the population continues to increase through in-migration. Currently, Singapore's population is 5.8 million, out of which almost 2 million are foreign workers. About one-tenth of the resident population are permanent residents, which usually indicates first-generation migrants. Thailand, Brunei, and Malaysia have the highest levels of international migrants in Southeast Asia, and most of these migrants have gone to cities (Kathiravelu & Wong, 2019). Most migration within national boundaries is from nonurban to urban areas, as these migrations are often economically driven. The share of population in urban areas of Southeast Asia stood at 41.8 percent in 2010 and is projected to reach 65 percent by 2050.

Table 4 Total Fertility Rate (TFR) of Selected Mega-Urban Regions of
Southeast Asia

City	Year	TFR of the Metropolitan Area	TFR of Country
Jakarta	1991	2.18	3.02
	2000	1.78	2.51
	2017	1.5 (2011)	2.34
Bangkok	1984–7	1.60	2.23
	1991	1.41	2.06
	2000	1.16	1.67
	2016	0.8	1.54
Metro Manila	1993	2.76	4.11
	2000	2.80	3.81
	2013	2.3	2.98
Ho Chi Minh City	1999	1.40	2.09
	2018	1.33	2.05
Yangon	2014	1.8	2.22
Vientiane	2011–12	2.0	2.98
Phnom Penh	2014	2	2.63
Brunei Darussalam	2018		1.8
Kuala Lumpur	2011	1.53	2.13
	2015	1.40	2.06
Singapore	1988	1.96	1.96
	2000	1.60	1.60
	2012	1.29	1.29

Sources: Douglass & Jones, 2008; MDHS, 2015-16; PSA and ICF International, 2014; Ministry of Health & Lao Statistics Bureau 2012; National Population and Family Planning Board et al., 2018; Jakarta Open Data, 2018; World Bank, 2019; Department of Statistics Singapore, 2020.

The significance of migration in urban development raises several issues, which, as for other marginalized groups, urge a deeper examination of real-life experiences beyond what statistics indicate. First, low-wage migrants are likely to become subjects of "structured inequalities" (Kathiravelu & Wong, 2019: 148). Low-wage migrants in Singapore who come to work in jobs that are considered "unskilled," such as domestic work, construction, and cleaning, are likely to have taken on high debts to finance their work placement through employment agencies. In general, low-wage migrants invest varying amounts of financial, social, and time resources to make it to the city before they start work. They then commonly receive low – if not the lowest – levels of income in the city, as low wages are one of the main reasons employers recruit from outside the city. Low income combines with nonresident status, which means they may not be entitled to various social benefits available to "permanent" residents in the city, such as education, healthcare, and income subsidies. These migrant-specific inequalities combine, too, with other social inequalities. For instance, the intersection of migration status and gender contributes to a gender wage gap, gender-based discrimination in hiring practices, and harassment in the workplace (Kathiravelu & Wong, 2019). Furthermore, as part of a transient population, migrants have fewer political rights in the city, such as to vote in local elections or endorse political candidates, and lack representation in the local parliament. The structure renders them dependent on sympathetic residents to advocate for their rights and interests.

Employment agencies extract labor from outside the city to serve as low-wage workers in the urban economy, although in cases of internal migration such recruitment may also be through existing social and personal networks between city residents and their nonurban counterparts. Migrants may also work in the "informal" economy through their social and personal networks in the city or in their residential enclaves (Simone & Pieterese, 2017). In such situations, migrants' legal protection depends on their employers. An informal economy profession as ordinary as street vending also comes with risks of legal repercussions and extortion from more powerful groups, including the authorities. While a top-down view can capture migrants' wage inequality, their efforts for economic survival in the city are impossible to capture without a view from below. Yet examining these efforts, as well as the approaches researchers use to study them, is important to understand the role of migration in urban development and to inform policies that address inequalities.

Second, urban migration in Southeast Asia consists not only of migration of low-wage workers but also of those in the "skilled workers" category. Both "skilled" and "unskilled" migrants are manifestations of global flows in urban development. Both face limitations in the city, such as restricted access to benefits that city residents are entitled to as well as to representation in the local government and parliament. "Skilled" migrants are usually better placed in terms of their economic status, occupying positions in the workplace the same as or even higher than those of citizens and other residents. In the global city paradigm, city governments usually aim to "attract investors, professionals and white-collar workers," who are the "skilled" migrants that enjoy elevated economic status (Kong, 2007: 386; Yeoh, 2005). Hence, the close link between urban development and migration in Southeast Asia has complex consequences for socioeconomic inequality in the city. Migrants may constitute both the low and high ends of the economic spectrum, but those at both poles experience limited "rights to the city," having been denied the right to change the city after their heart's desire (Baas, 2019: 141; Harvey, 2003: 939). Understanding the different experiences of migrants in different socioeconomic classes, how their presence affects urban life in general, and how they interact with the existing population requires perspectives from the ground.

Furthermore, migration as part of urban development is not just about movement across territory but also about connections. Migrants embody experiences of migrating and being in-between while also being part of social and cultural life in two places. Through his work on migrants' mobility between Batam and Singapore, Johan Lindquist (2008) introduced the concept of an "emotional economy" that connects the home and the space of migration. Migration itself is a gendered phenomenon: in the *rantau* tradition in Indonesia, for instance, it is a coming-of-age ritual for men to migrate out in search of better opportunities, with the expectation of their becoming more mature and established and therefore higher-status. From this perspective, migration may or may not entail a permanent move to the city but is rather a form of connection between two geographies. Therefore, another related tradition is the regular return home, commonly identified as *mudik* in Indonesia or *balikbayan* in the Philippines. The connection between the home and the space of migration renders migration a circular phenomenon rather than a linear progression toward the city.

A direct consequence of this circular aspect of migration is the intensification of geographical networks. Physical infrastructure to connect the city to the homes of migrants becomes an important part of urban development, mobility between those places becomes an important part of the urban economy, and communication across geographies intensifies. The reality for migrants of being in between permanence and transience also has social and cultural consequences: How do migrants settle in the city, how do they form social networks in the city, and how do they use urban spaces as part of the population? In the case of Singapore, there are areas that are more popular among some migrant groups than others, and each area may be specific to one migrant group, as demonstrated by the popularity of Little India for South Asian migrant workers, Lucky Plaza for Filipina domestic workers, and Little Burma at Peninsula Plaza for Burmese workers (Ferzacca, 2022; Sinha, 2018; Yeoh & Huang, 1998).

4.2.4 Heterogeneity and "In-between"

As industrialization and massive population increases have occurred in a condensed time and space in most cities in Southeast Asia, much of that population growth has been through in-migration. A closer examination of cities in Southeast Asia enriches discussion of the role of migration in population growth and of the social-cultural dynamics of a heterogeneous urban society. Wirth (1938) argued that it is difficult for city dwellers to know each other personally when the population increases, and hence they structure their communication "through indirect mediums." On the one hand, this delegation is important in a society with a blasé or "impersonal, superficial, transitory, and segmental" attitude (Wirth, 1938: 12; Simmel, 1903), leading to the bureaucratization of city management. On the other hand, a grounded vantage point shows reality to be more mixed than Wirth suggests. Many migrants have come to Southeast Asian cities through preexisting contacts and, given the scarcity of affordable housing, formed enclaves of people from the same background (Kusno, 2014; Shatkin, 2004). Studies in Yangon, for instance, show residents forming hybrid communities of different ethnicities, reshaping ethnic and religious boundaries through informal housing provisions amidst the state's inability to offer affordable housing (Roberts, 2019). These enclaves are also likely be the first point of entry into jobs in the city. The continuation of relatively close-knit communities as enclaves in the urban fabric demonstrates that social relations in the city are not all impersonal.

The ethnic enclave pattern was also observable in cities of North America, such as in Chicago in the early twentiethth century, as European migrants from World War I settled in. Wirth observed such patterns as he claimed that different parts of the city featured specialized functions and that "persons of homogenous status and needs unwittingly drift into, consciously select, or are forced by circumstances into, the same area" (1938: 15). More recent studies in Southeast Asia remind us that settling into enclaves does not protect migrants from being subjected to the "modern" aspirations the larger society attaches to the image of the city (Elinoff, 2018). As a result, settlement enclaves became a means of social and economic survival for those comprising the second class or lower in the city, while those in the first class represent the "global city" image: they partake of "croissants and opera" rather than "bread and circuses" (Yeoh, 2005).

The pursuit of global city status, along with the role of cities as nodes in the global economy, has led to various modes of developmentalism. In Vietnam, modernization and global integration came with *doi moi* (economic reform), leading to years of rapid economic growth and urbanization that specified the goal of "integration with the global economy" (Tran, 2019). Pen Sereypagna's (2018) description of this phenomenon in Phnom Penh illustrates how developmentalism relates to the image of a modernized, global city: "The micro-economies of street vendors, stalls and small-scale commercial streets are being eliminated in the face of new rules and regulations, new shopping malls and new ideals of cleanliness and hygiene" (Sereypagna, 2018: 47). Enclaves of migrants are also subjected to requirements of beauty and order to align with the demands of the global economy, causing some of these enclaves to evolve to embrace tourism (Figure 5). These transformations are consistent with the accumulation of "cultural capital" in a global city, which affects people, products, and places (Kong, 2007: 384).

While the density of inhabitants in the city might encourage social partitioning, settlement enclaves in Southeast Asia can sustain close, personal interactions, especially in relatively old settlements that have evolved over a considerably long time. For example, research by the Southeast Asia Neighborhoods Network (SEANNET) has consistently found that personal interactions among neighbors can persist in spite of development pressures and might foster platforms to negotiate for or against those pressures (UKNA, 2020). In Surabaya, Indigenous urban settlements known as *kampung* have obtained official acknowledgment as important to sustain, since "if *kampung* disappears, so will the culture [of the city]" (Silas, 2020). In fact, the image of the *kampung* in other cities has been as an area opposed to the notion of progress. Many such communities have faced forced eviction in the name

Figure 5 Arab Town in the city of Bangkok, which has evolved into a neighborhood that offers restaurants, mini-marts, and other functions to support tourism.
Source: Author, 2020.

of development, but their persistence in a city like Surabaya exemplifies a less dichotomous relationship between *kampung* and urban development (Peeters, 2013). An anthropological lens on the city allows one to observe the endurance of close social interactions that make apparent "that elites and various kinds of authorities *only appear* to have a monopoly on envisioning more lasting (urban) futures *and* that ordinary city-makers and/or religion-makers are important players as well" (Sinha, 2018: 264). Most cities in Southeast Asia have these variations in dense urban living, as the built environment has continuously mixed impersonal megaprojects with settlements marked by close-knit urban fabric.

4.3 Groundedness and Multi-Scalar Thinking

Although this section has focused on the limitations of official datasets and the importance of a grounded perspective in studying urban development, it is important to avoid pitting one against the other. Motivating the emphasis on groundedness is the insufficient consideration of everyday life experiences of urban inhabitants, especially of marginalized groups, in most official urban development planning thus far. The fact that official data may miss certain populations, or perceive city boundaries differently or unrealistically, complicates comparison, but qualitative triangulation, based on grounded knowledge of at least some sites, can help test for the limitations of the data, to allow scholars and policy practitioners alike to adjust accordingly. An awareness of the extent to which power inequality has obscured the experiences of marginalized groups in urban development encourages studies that challenge unequal structures. Without such awareness, urban research may perpetuate unjust social structures, as technocratic planning continues to be dominant in economies under global capitalism.

Developing suitable research methods to study socially fragmented landscapes, with full knowledge of the colonial and postcolonial contexts of urban development and awareness of development-induced injustices, is as important as identifying pertinent research topics. The significance of groundedness is that it recognizes the value of the human agency of marginalized groups; they are not mere objects of research but active actors in urban development. Inherent in this understanding is the recognition that urban development has perpetuated injustices. Since studying urban development in Southeast Asia may result in one's becoming part of the urban development process, it is imperative for scholars of urban Southeast Asia to start with clear objectives: Why are we studying urbanization, with whom, and for whom? With the range of power inequalities that shadow and propel urban developments in Southeast Asia, the "who" question is particularly important. Embedded in clarifying the objectives of urban scholars of Southeast Asia is the awareness that urban landscapes are representations of those unequal powers. Of key importance is for researchers to maintain a critical perspective, given the closeness between academic studies and their real-life implications in cities of Southeast Asia.

5 Political Ecology and Environmental Justice

Bringing insights from human agency and political life as seen from below into urban policymaking allows city planners to make social justice a crucial part of development strategies. The inequalities and patterns of marginalization discussed thus far imply the need for a new focus not just in studies of urban development but also in shaping the realities of urbanization. Centering a concern for justice acknowledges the impossibility of "leveling" a heterogeneous and socially unequal urban society.

Taking justice seriously as an objective in planning and studying cities also requires broadening one's vantage point to view urban development as a set of processes that affect areas beyond city boundaries. The fixation of urban development on the convenience and comfort of cities comes together with enshrining cities as centers of social and economic life. Cities become spaces of accumulation of wealth and power, as cities turn out to be sites of development decisions and to be places that absorb resources from rural areas. Compounded by planners' violations of master plans in pursuit of profit-making endeavors, the urban bias that results is clearly observable in its consequences for environmental sustainability. Environmental degradation resulting from unbalanced urban development occurs both in cities proper and in places that are well outside the metropolitan area but are still economically and ecologically linked to city-centric initiatives. Sprawling mega-urban regions also give rise to environmental challenges, since national environmental policies are often "too broad to effectively cope with the diversity of urban eco-systems," and the tension between development expectations and the need to protect ecosystems persists in most places (McGee & Shaharudin, 2016: 511).

In examining urbanization impacts beyond borders, a focus on justice refers not only to distribution of benefits, resources, and costs but also to processes of decision-making and ideological contests regarding urban development. Hence again the need for groundedness in urban development research to ensure attention to marginalized groups, both in the process and in the resulting outcomes of development. Questions of social and environmental justice, therefore, become lenses through which to study urban development's impacts on different social groups, recognizing that race, ethnicity, and gender are inseparable from economic class in the social construction of those social groups.

5.1 Political Ecology

A political ecology framework is useful in critically analyzing how political economy interacts with ecology and examining connections between social and environmental inequalities. Urban political ecology looks at the unequal distribution of power in urban spaces to analyze the differential impacts of policy decisions among social, political, and economic groups (Marks, 2019). Rather than focusing only on powerful actors in urban development, political ecology demands a closer look at power inequality and, consequently, is critical of development processes, given their impacts on those in the margins.

Scholars of Southeast Asia's urban development have used an urban political ecology framework to scrutinize development's impacts on nature and on groups that are most affected by development-induced natural degradation. For example, a political ecology framework to analyze flooding would fault not a natural cause but political and economic decision-making regarding urban development. The framework is also helpful in shaping a critical view of technocratic-infrastructural approaches to urban issues, seeing these as resulting from political and economic decisions made in contexts of unequal power relations. In the case of Jakarta, for example, while politicians and citizens blame urban poor settlements for floods, a political ecology analysis considers the urban poor as a disadvantaged group that is marginalized in urban development decision-making processes. Their settlements are at the receiving end of the negative impacts of those developments, while the big developers that cause environmental degradation can afford more protection for themselves against the floods (Padawangi & Douglass, 2015). As a closer examination of flooding, waste, and pollution makes clear, a political ecology perspective shows that urban development, as human interventions into natural ecologies, brings differential impacts to people situated in different social, political, and economic configurations across the urban landscape.

5.1.1 Flooding

Flooding is both the most common urban disaster in Southeast Asia and also one the most closely linked to urban development (Padawangi & Douglass, 2015). A political ecology approach to understand flooding in relation to Southeast Asia's urbanization points to the role of urban and national politicians' interest-laden decisions as the root of uneven vulnerability to floods (Marks, 2019; DiGregorio, 2015). Cambodia, Malaysia, and Thailand are the Southeast Asian countries in which the threat of flooding is greatest, although it is also a threat in other countries in the region (Kim and Bui, 2019). Most Southeast Asia cities with populations of more than 1 million have experienced flooding incidents more than once since 2012 (Table 5). Jakarta and Metro Manila – both among the world's top twenty mega-urban regions by population size – are especially critically unprepared (Douglass, 2010). Development-induced urban flooding stems from the reduction of green areas in cities and their surroundings, degradation of the river system for riverine cities, and land subsidence in coastal cities (Padawangi, 2019; Marks, 2019; Kim & Bui, 2019). Climate change exacerbates these development-induced hazards, particularly for cities that are in typhoon paths and coastal areas (Kim & Bui, 2019).

Building physical infrastructure, such as levees and dams, is still a common strategy to mitigate flooding in cities in Southeast Asia. The city government of Jakarta, for example, chose to build levees along its main river, Ciliwung, in hopes of curing Jakarta's chronic flooding. This strategy required that authorities forcefully evict communities to build the levees. While levees may alleviate floods' impact, they may also both give a false sense of security and reduce green areas in the city. Widespread flooding in Jakarta in early 2020, including in areas that are purportedly protected by the river levees, is evidence of the weakness of such a strategy.

Urban development may also cause flooding and disaster risks elsewhere, as demonstrated in the case of Thailand's reliance on electricity produced in Laos. Laos' aspiration to become the "Battery of Asia" symbolically frames the various hydropower projects the country is developing along the Mekong River. Laos has signed an agreement with Thailand to supply 9,000 megawatts (MW) of power to Thailand by 2036, although it had only managed to supply 2,100 MW as of 2018. Most of Laos' hydropower-produced electricity in Thailand eventually goes into the transmission grid in and around Bangkok (Marks & Zhang, 2018: 300). The sale of electricity for mostly urban development in Thailand generates national revenue for Laos, but the infrastructure involved imposes disaster risks for the areas in which the dams have been built. The example of the collapse of the Xe-Pian Xe-Namnoy hydropower project's dam in July 2018 – killing 34, causing 100 people to be missing, and displacing thousands of residents from thirteen villages – is a reminder of the risk that these rural areas shoulder by being located near hydropower dams (The Nation, 2018).

5.1.2 Waste and Pollution

Environmental losses are rarely included in official calculations of urban development costs and benefits. While urban development may bring benefits to some, its environmental costs for others may extend well beyond cities' administrative boundaries or even national borders, as natural landscapes have

Table 5 Flood risk of cities with over 1 million population in Southeast Asia

COUNTRY	CITY	COASTAL	FLOOD RISK
Cambodia	Phnom Penh	Yes (riverine)	High
Indonesia	Bandar Lampung	Yes	High
	Bandung	No	Low
	Batam	Yes	High
	Bogor	No	Low
	Denpasar	Yes	High
	Jakarta	Yes	High
	Makassar	Yes	High
	Malang	No	Low
	Medan	Yes	High
	Palembang	Yes (riverine)	High
	Pekan Baru	Yes (riverine)	High
	Samarinda	Yes (riverine)	High
	Semarang	Yes	High
	Surabaya	Yes	High
	Tasikmalaya	No	Low
Laos	Vientiane	Yes (riverine)	High
Malaysia	Johor Bahru	Yes (riverine)	High
	Kuala Lumpur	Yes	High
	Penang	Yes	High
Myanmar	Mandalay	Yes (riverine)	High
	Nay Pyi Taw	No	Low
	Yangon	Yes (riverine)	High
Philippines	Cebu City	Yes	High
	Davao City	Yes	High
	Manila	Yes	High
	Zamboanga City	Yes	High
Singapore	Singapore	Yes	High
Thailand	Bangkok	Yes	High
	Samut Prakan	Yes	High
Vietnam	Bien Hoa	Yes (riverine)	High
	Can Tho	Yes (riverine)	High
	Da Nang	Yes	High
	Hai Phong	Yes	High
	Hanoi	Yes (riverine)	High
	Ho Chi Minh City	Yes	High

"Low" indicates no flooding; "high" indicates more than one flooding incident in years 2012–17. These are officially reported data and may not include all actual incidents.
Source: Kim & Bui, 2019.

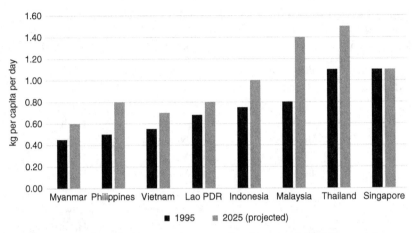

Figure 6 Projected urban waste generation in some ASEAN countries. **Source:** UNEP, 2017.

their own terrains and systems. A case in point is the waste management issues that Southeast Asia's cities commonly face. Southeast Asia generates 1.14 kg per capita in municipal solid waste per day, consisting mostly of healthcare waste, electronic waste, industrial waste, and construction and demolition waste (UNEP, 2017). Within Southeast Asia, Indonesia generates the highest amount, at more than 60 million tons per year, followed by Thailand at almost 30 million tons (Figure 6). These quantities have surged during the COVID-19 pandemic that started in 2020, as can be observed from the increase of plastic waste, heightened reliance on online shopping and food delivery, and a significant rise in medical waste (Kojima et al., 2020).

Most cities in the region rely primarily on open dumping and open burning to manage solid waste (Table 6). Singapore uses incineration, but it faces a shortage of space for ashes, which still need to go to a landfill. In general, recycling rates are still relatively low, and most cities depend on the informal sector to recover recyclable materials from open landfills (UNEP, 2017). Open landfills, usually situated on the outskirts of or outside cities, have environmental and public-health implications for those areas and communities. In other words, wealth accumulation in cities produces unequally distributed negative impacts, particularly among less-wealthy populations.

Such a situation raises critical questions about environmental justice. The insufficient capacities of governments to uphold regulations and the willingness of interest-laden state actors to externalize environmental costs add to the difficulties of alleviating unequal and unjust situations. Almost all countries in Southeast Asia have some relevant environmental policies, regulatory

Table 6 Recycling rate and municipal solid waste treatment technology

Country	Source Segregation	Collection Rate (Urban)	Recycling Rate	Treatment/Disposal				
				Composting	Incineration	Sanitary Landfill	Open Dump	Open Burning
Brunei Darussalam	<50%	90%	15%			✓	✓	
Cambodia	<50%	80%	<50%	✓		✓	✓	✓
Indonesia	<50%	56–75%	<50%	✓	✓	✓	✓	✓
Lao PDR	<50%	40–70%	<50%	✓		✓	✓	✓
Malaysia	<50%	>70%	50–60% (Metal, Paper, Plastic) Others (<50%)		✓	✓	✓	
Myanmar	50%		70% (Metal, Paper, Plastic)		✓	✓	✓	
Philippines	50–70%	40–90%	20–33% (Paper) 30–70% (Aluminium) 20–58% (Other Metals) 23–42% (Plastic) 28–60% (Glass)	✓		✓	✓	

Table 6 (cont.)

Country	Source Segregation	Collection Rate (Urban)	Recycling Rate	Treatment/Disposal				
				Composting	Incineration	Sanitary Landfill	Open Dump	Open Burning
Singapore	70%	>90%	50–60% (Paper, Horticulture) >90% (Iron, Construction & Demolition, Used Slag) >80% (Scrap Tire) >80% (Wood) >50% (Others) Overall: 60%		✓	✓	✓	
Thailand	<50%	>80%	>90% (Metal) 50–60% (Paper, Construction) <50% (Others)	✓	✓	✓	✓	
Vietnam	<50%	80–82%	>90% (Metal) >70% (Plastic, E-waste) 50% (Paper) <50% (Others)	✓		✓	✓	

Source: UNEP, 2017.

frameworks, and strategies on the national level, but lack of coordination between different levels of government and policymakers results in difficulty with implementation, a situation that echoes the inconsistent implementation of urban master plans.

Handling of liquid waste has also been challenging. Disposal of untreated liquid waste and wastewater, both industrial and domestic (Steinberg, 2007), directly into rivers or other nearby bodies of water causes degradation of river water quality across the region. Many rivers in large cities in the region – such as the Chao Phraya in Bangkok, the Pasig River in Metro Manila, the Ciliwung River in Jakarta, and the Saigon River in Ho Chi Minh City – have been declared biologically dead, nearly biologically dead, or heavily contaminated for the portions that run through the city (Bello, 2016; Johnson and Simonette, 2019; Padawangi et al., 2016). River pollution reflects the problem of urban development's turning cities' backs to rivers, causing rivers to become sewers and open drains rather than natural resources for water and food.

Air pollution is another important and often overlooked issue for Southeast Asia's urban development. Brunei Darussalam has the highest CO_2 emissions per capita in Southeast Asia (Figure 7). However, when computed based on the concentration of PM 2.5 particles,[2] Indonesia is the most polluted country, with an average of 45.3 µg/m³, which is in the range the WHO identifies as "unhealthy for sensitive groups" (IQAir, 2018). The most polluted city in Southeast Asia is Jakarta, Indonesia, followed by Hanoi in Vietnam. However, ten cities in Thailand dominate the list of the top fifteen most polluted cities (Table 7). Cities in the Philippines dominate among those in the region with the cleanest air, interestingly, with cities in Metro Manila, such as Valenzuela, Parañaque, the old Manila, Makati, Quezon City, Mandaluyong, and Las Pinas among the top fifteen cleanest. Singapore is also in the list of the top fifteen cities with the best air quality, despite having to endure regular haze from forest fires in the region.

Nevertheless, the WHO ranks the air quality in only four cities in Southeast Asia as "good" – that is, with an annual average of PM 2.5 particles of less than 12 µg/m³. This means that almost all cities in Southeast Asia fall short of WHO targets. In Indonesia, for instance, besides Jakarta's being the most polluted city in the region, seasonal open burning of agricultural land damages Indonesia's air quality as a whole and affects the air quality of neighboring countries. The country's dependency on coal for energy generation for development needs (Antara, 2019) – use of coal-powered electricity is projected to increase from

---

[2] PM 2.5 are fine particles that are smaller than human hair. Scientists have linked prolonged exposure to PM 2.5 pollution to heart and lung diseases that may lead to premature death.

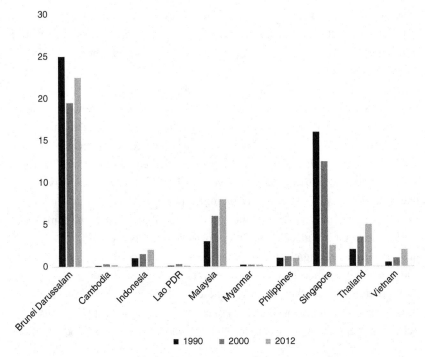

Figure 7 CO_2 emissions, in metric tons per capita.
Source: UNEP, 2017.

25 percent in 2015 to more than 30 percent in 2025 – also raises concern over air quality and health impacts from coal burning.

5.1.3 Political Ecology as Urban Development Critique

Political ecology's critical approach to many aspects of urban development that cause and exacerbate social inequalities positions it as a critique of capitalist development. Therefore, this perspective goes against the interests of political and economic elites who profit from urban development projects. As Mayer (2020: 46) says, of scholars who take a critical approach, "One challenge which critical social scientists have always faced has grown bigger: neither policy makers nor corporate elites seem to be paying much attention to their research findings." Furthermore, political ecology analysis goes beyond the administrative boundaries of the city, which may not be attractive for policymakers or politicians who have a specific interest in appealing to their voters. The usefulness of a political ecology framework in achieving sustainable environment is clear, but its appeal may thus be limited among both urban politicians and influential economic actors.

Table 7 The fifteen most polluted cities and fifteen cleanest cities in Southeast Asia, based on average PM 2.5 particles concentration

		Most Polluted Regional Cities				Cleanest Regional Cities	
Rank	Country	City	2018 Average PM 2.5	Rank	Country	City	2018 Average PM 2.5
1	Indonesia	Jakarta	45.3	1	Philippines	Calamba	9.3
2	Vietnam	Hanoi	40.8	2	Philippines	Valenzuela	9.9
3	Thailand	Samut Sakhon	39.8	3	Philippines	Carmona	10.9
4	Thailand	Nakhon Ratchasima	37.6	4	Thailand	Satun	11.3
5	Thailand	Tha Bo	37.2	5	Philippines	Parañaque	12.2
6	Thailand	Saraburi	32.6	6	Philippines	Davao City	12.6
7	Philippines	Meycauyan City	32.4	7	Philippines	Makati	13.7
8	Thailand	Samut Prakan	32.2	8	Philippines	Manila	14.3
9	Thailand	Ratchaburi	32.2	9	Philippines	Mandaluyong	14.5
10	Thailand	Mae Sot	32.2	10	Singapore	Singapore	14.8
11	Philippines	Caloocan	31.4	11	Thailand	Narathiwat	15.2
12	Thailand	Si Maha Phot	30.9	12	Philippines	Balanga	16.1
13	Thailand	Pai	29.4	13	Philippines	Quezon City	17.5
14	Thailand	Chon Buri	27.3	14	Thailand	Nan	17.6
15	Vietnam	Ho Chi Minh City	26.9	15	Philippines	Las Pinas	17.9

The World Health Organization (WHO) sets a target of less than 10 µg/m³, while defining "good" air quality levels as 0–12 µg/m³. The range of 12.1–35.4 µg/m³ is "moderate," while 35.5–55.4 µg/m³ is "unhealthy for sensitive groups."
Source: IQAir, 2018.

5.2 Urban Social Movements

Given the differential impacts of the social and environmental consequences of Southeast Asia's urban development on various groups, social and environmental justice continue to be pertinent. The focus of environmental justice on the relationship among social, political, and economic inequalities addresses the extent to which urban development harms/damages/reduces quality of life, especially among marginalized groups. Social justice literatures likewise critique capitalist urbanization, by assessing the impact of urban development for different economic classes in the city (Harvey, 1973). Both these literatures consider principles, processes, and outcomes of justice, as well as intergenerational and intragenerational justice.

Including principles and processes of justice in evaluating development leads scholars to resistance groups and urban social movements. Since many Southeast Asian governments implement top-down master plans inconsistently, and since even those plans that governments follow are subject to change, such plans can be contested. Urban development challenges present issues around which civil society groups can organize and mobilize, including through coalition-building among diverse social groups and political actors. Some, though not all, also build coalitions with political candidates during election seasons. Powerful political elites and economic actors may make use of such opportunities to assert their interests, but civil society groups can also seize upon them. The possibilities for civil society groups to push for their agendas to be included in master plans or other urban policies vary across cities as well as provincial and national contexts.

In general, social and environmental issues offer potential for civil society organization and mobilization. While the urban poor have become a political force in urban development in Southeast Asia, their level of and opportunities for organizing are still uneven across contexts. Furthermore, community organizing that is based on delivery of basic services and needs also has its limitations, because it mixes pragmatic and ideological concerns. In fact, urban issues generally combine such dimensions, even if they are not directly related to basic services and needs fulfilment. If a social movement is successful in achieving its pragmatic concerns, the next question would be whether ideological concerns remain to sustain its organizing and mobilizing as a political force.

Environmental movements are examples of movements that may not directly relate to basic services and needs fulfilment, but still have both pragmatic and ideological aspects. As environmental issues and their effects on quality of life become more obvious, civil society groups have emerged in the region to engage in grassroots efforts to address these challenges – though some groups are long-standing. The Nature Society Singapore, for example, established in 1921 as the Singapore Natural History Society, has successfully advocated for more serious attention to the city's natural environment and biodiversity in formal policies. Some of the most well-known of its advocacy efforts were its proposal for a nature conservation area at Sungei Buloh in 1988 and the conservation of Chek Jawa mudflats in 2001 (Nature Society, 2020). Recently, the Nature Society has also advocated for the conservation of the Green Corridor, the land that was formerly occupied by the Singapore–Malaysia railway. The case of the Nature Society in Singapore shows that even a city-state that has a relatively more controlled and structured master plan leaves space for civil society groups to assert their concerns regarding urban development.

It remains to be seen whether urban social movements in Southeast Asia can mobilize to redirect the politics of urban development away from technocratic approaches. These social movements actively play roles in urban development politics through strategies that include advocacy, capacity-building, lobbying, and coalition-building with a range of political actors. Their emergence may be influenced by democratization and political reform, such as in the cases of Indonesia and the Philippines, but civil society organizations persist and mobilize throughout the region at various levels and scales. The incomplete control of top-down urban governance in most of Southeast Asia, while posing challenges for upholding regulations and opening avenues for political lobbying, also presents a political opportunity for grassroots activists to raise awareness of injustices and to appropriate spaces for empowerment and agency – a process to which the next section, on Southeast Asia's urban futures, turns.

6 Southeast Asia's Urban Futures

Having discussed the historical and the contemporary, we turn now to possible futures for urban development in Southeast Asia. The social inequalities of the past and present affect aspirations for the future. Groups in unequal social settings may have different priorities, but they still "may have common – or at least overlapping – visions of aspirational futures" (Bunnell, 2018: 11).

Three distinctive ways of studying Southeast Asia's urban futures offer useful insight. The first is through the aspirations of different actors in urban development. Their positions in the political and social structures of urban societies affect these actors' aspirations, but at the same time all share spaces in and imaginations of the city. The second is through considering technological advancements in the city, which affect both policymakers and citizens as these innovations become more pervasive in everyday life. The third is through grassroots activism and alternative development initiatives that provide glimpses into ways to move away from the mainstream.

6.1 Aspirations

Studies of urbanization in Southeast Asia rarely address aspirations, despite their importance for many urban development-related phenomena (Bunnell et al., 2019): they "drive urban transformation, usually incrementally but sometimes also in revolutionary ways" (Goh et al., 2015: 291). Aspiration, explains Arjun Appadurai (2004), is not just an individual's desire or choice for a desired future but a "system of ideas" that comprises perceptions of "good life, health and happiness" (Bunnell et al., 2019: 54). Aspiration is both individual and social-structural; it may originate in the realm of the subaltern or of the powerful. The relationship between the marginalized and the powerful is not always neatly in opposition, as there are also actors who advocate, mediate, or intervene to produce alternative aspirations (Goh et al., 2015). In the urban context, aspirations for a good city and a good urban life reflect a socially constructed system of ideas that may be specifically grounded but is also influenced by images from an idealized elsewhere at the global scale.

Even as it inspires aspirations for a better future life, the city can still be a site that limits marginalized groups – such as the urban poor, including migrants – from achieving such aspirations. Limitations in accessing job opportunities and affordable housing are common hurdles that marginalize migrants in the city. Those who serve as low-wage workers in industries, for instance, may experience labor exploitation and gender discrimination. Nevertheless, the city can also become a space to encounter other urban actors who could work together to resist injustices. Resistance against oppressive situations and actors can be covert or open, depending on the situation, but migrants and members of other marginalized groups may transform their lot through such a process of struggle (see Warouw, 2019). Indeed, besides being centers of wealth accumulation, cities are also possible sites of labor activism, as well as of housing and human rights advocacy.

The presence of top-down technocratic governance and the global market forces that drive big infrastructural and commercial developments in the city affect urban aspirations of actors from state to grassroots (Bunnell & Goh, 2012; Ghertner, 2010). The historical linking of urban development and nation-building is the archetype for how the developmental state might manage and cultivate aspirations across social and political groups, moving forward. Both large infrastructure projects and provision of basic services reflect the abilities of the state and its image of the good life, to be achieved through urban development. To go even further back in history, the role of cities as ceremonial centers prepares them to serve as stages for idealized and therefore monumental images of societal life. Studies of communities threatened with eviction in cities in Southeast Asia, such as in Ho Chi Minh City, Metro Manila, and Jakarta, indicate that even residents' images of a "good city" idealize monumental buildings and beautiful new developments (Harms, 2012; Shatkin, 2004; Padawangi, 2018c). The urban poor may have "the capacity to aspire," yet they remain "pragmatically modest in their hopes, as they [are] also aware of the necessity to rely on other actors in the city, whose interests may not align with their own, to fulfil their aspirations" (Padawangi, 2018c: 215).

The ambitious state's role in cultivating aspirations and setting criteria for what constitutes an ideal city comes through most clearly in plans for new cities. In Phnom Penh, for example, the Diamond Island project emptied out space by evicting farmers and fishermen to create an "international city." The plan operationalized an idea of "one city from around the world" with an eclectic mix of facsimiles of European, Singaporean, and American architectural icons to represent "luxurious prosperity" (Yamada, 2019: 313). In the case of Myanmar, the military-controlled government has built a completely new city, Nay Pyi Taw, as a new capital, to replace Yangon (which they claimed was "too congested"). Officially becoming Myanmar's capital city in 2006, Nay Pyi Taw has become the new command center of the military (Preecharushh, 2010). Government aspirations for a more controlled space are also apparent in the proposal to move the capital of Indonesia from the congested and regularly flooded Jakarta to a completely new city in East Kalimantan. The winning design for the new capital city highlights idealized concepts of green city design and sustainability, framed as a "forest city" (Henschke, 2020). The new city design also features a smart-city command center facility that represents planning and control, as opposed to the usual messy city (Henschke & Utama, 2020). The government claims the new city to be the antithesis, and to a certain extent also an antidote, to urban development challenges generally in Southeast Asia. But these official and ideal visions rely on clearing existing populations and livelihoods – for instance, farmers and fishermen from Diamond Island in Phnom Penh – much as for other mega-projects in the region.

Addressing aspirations in Southeast Asia's urban development highlights the importance of human imaginings of a better life and a good city – and how both context and power relations shape these (Bunnell et al., 2019). Focusing on aspirations offers a useful perspective for uncovering nuances in and influences on visions of urban futures; these visions are not fixed but continuously negotiated, and they involve struggles, resistance, and advocacy. Such dynamics may vary from one city to another, depending on relationships among government, civil society, and market actors. In whatever proportion, these actors will continue to carve out space to shape urban development in the future.

6.2 Infrastructure and Technological Advancements

Urban development relies on infrastructure and technological advancements to deliver the image of progress, and sometimes futuristic expectations, to the built environment. These infrastructural and technological advancements are also part of a circuit of capital and wealth accumulation, while influencing residents' imaginations of a "good city." Some of these technologies are pervasive in everyday urban life; city residents often take them for granted, although these technologies inherently preserve power inequality in urban development.

6.2.1 Ubiquitous Transportation Technologies

Modes of transportation influence the organization of urban spaces and neighborhoods in cities in Southeast Asia. Rapid urban development in Southeast Asia started along with the boom in automobile and oil production, which affected the scale of spaces in cities accordingly. Studies from Bangkok, Metro Manila, and Jakarta noted a period of "rapid motorization and hyper-congestion" that started with the focus on road expansion in the 1970s (Chalermpong, 2019). This pattern is most observable in primate cities in the region, but development of secondary cities also prioritized access for automobiles as the most recent transportation technology at the time of industrialization. Automobile-oriented development continued well into the 1990s. Even in Singapore – the city in Southeast Asia that is most often hailed for its exemplary public transportation system, with more than 7.5 million trips taken per day (LTA, 2020) – urban development, distances, and road sizes are at the scale of automobiles, which has also caused automobiles to remain the fastest mode of transportation from point to point.

Over the past two decades, several large cities in Southeast Asia have expanded rail-based and other forms of integrated public transportation. The Bangkok Transit System (BTS) began operation in 1999 and gradually expanded to 109.4 km with seventy-seven stations in 2018 (Chalermpong, 2019). Metro Manila also launched its first rail transit system in 1999; by 2019 it had expanded to 124.4 km of tracks with forty-nine mass rapid transit (MRT) and light rail transit (LRT) stations. Jakarta launched its first MRT line in 2019, consisting of 20.1 km of railway track and thirteen stations, in addition to the commuter rail system that started in 2000 and by 2017 was serving 1 million passengers per day (Andapita, 2019). Jakarta is also known for its bus rapid transit (BRT) system, which started operation in 2003 and has grown into the world's longest BRT system, covering 230.9 km of bus routes.

Development of new transportation modes, while providing alternatives to automobiles, does not reverse the trend of auto-oriented urban sprawl (Chalermpong, 2019). Rail-based transit systems in Bangkok, Metro Manila, and Jakarta, as well as Jakarta's BRT, have reasonably high ridership for their capacity. However, high ridership of public transportation does not automatically stop urban sprawl. The rail transit system in Bangkok induced more real estate development around train stations, but 14 percent of units were purchased as second homes (Chalermpong, 2019). Moreover, land use and land cover data of Bangkok Metropolitan Region show continuous expansion of built-up areas over the years that is still projected to continue (Losiri et al., 2016). While public transportation systems are much needed in cities of Southeast Asia, their introduction as late additions to sprawling cities that have existing dependencies on automobiles, with spaces at corresponding scales, would be unlikely to change urban development trends and main modes of transportation. Traffic congestion in these large cities is still bad despite their public transportation improvements. Rather, the new transit systems provide alternatives to commuters, but if market-driven development continues, the city's transportation networks will remain congested.

6.2.2 Information and Communication Technologies

Development of information and communication technologies in Southeast Asia's cities is important to urban infrastructural and cultural transformation. Most recently, many cities in Southeast Asia have latched onto the use of new technologies, together comprising a "smart cities" model, for efficient urban management (Table 8). The smart city paradigm relies on relatively advanced communication technology to deliver information and services, and it usually operates based on infrastructural capacity to store, manage, and retrieve data in a compressed time (Hollands, 2008). For example, gathering data on bus frequency and passenger travel patterns assists policymakers in designing new routes or altering existing ones. The large amount of data, collected and analyzed with the help of new technologies, is expected to assist city planners and other government authorities in making relatively quick decisions.

Technological aspirations related to urban development are not new in Southeast Asia. Monumental projects, such as Malaysia's Multimedia Super Corridor and Singapore's IT2000, have featured technology to address urban

Table 8 List of twenty-six pilot cities in the current ASEAN Smart Cities Network (ASCN)

Country	City
Brunei Darussalam	Bandar Seri Begawan
Cambodia	Battambang
	Phnom Penh
	Siem Reap
Lao PDR	Luang Prabang
	Vientiane
Indonesia	Banyuwangi
	DKI Jakarta
	Makassar
Malaysia	Johor Bahru
	Kota Kinabalu
	Kuala Lumpur
	Kuching
Myanmar	Mandalay
	Nay Pyi Taw
	Yangon
Philippines	Cebu
	Davao
	Metro Manila
Singapore	Singapore
Thailand	Bangkok
	Chon Buri
	Phuket
Vietnam	Da Nang
	Hanoi
	Ho Chi Minh City

Source: ASCN, 2018.

challenges and to solve problems. Recently, the ASEAN Smart City Network (ASCN) that was launched at the World Cities Summit in 2018 has invoked similar goals. Comprising twenty-six cities across the region, the ASCN aims to pursue a "high quality of life, competitive economy, and sustainable environment" by using technological and digital tools (ASCN, 2018: 3). One of the initiatives in the network is a provision for "matchmaking" city governments with private sector "solution providers" and "multilateral banks" as financiers (ASCN, 2018: 7). Such high-tech solutions require governments to have industry partners to provide platforms to digitally manage services and infra-structure in cities, including use of data collection tools such as cameras, sensors, and mobile phones. Usually the industry partners who can provide such tools are large international players such as IBM and Siemens. In other words, the Smart City agenda is a new entry point for a profit-making, multi-national private sector to expand their markets to city governments and citizens who are increasingly dependent on these technologies to get information needed to facilitate a more convenient urban life.

While the social science literature on smart cities has offered critical perspec-tives on the fascination with technology in urban management, these criticisms seem to have found little traction among policymakers on the implementation side in Southeast Asia. Scholars have raised questions about privacy issues in the use of big data for smart city projects, about data security, and about the ethics of data collection. Scholars have also criticized the widespread use of CCTV cameras to monitor movements as embodying a modern-day Panopticon (Foucault, 1975; Norris, 2005). The focus on convenience in city living drives the implementation of the smart city concept in Southeast Asia further from its initial premise of supporting human resources, social life, and economic growth (Allwinkle & Cruickshank, 2011), let alone addressing ethical concerns. Features of an all-seeing control room in city halls as part of the smart city agenda (Figure 8) also indicate a form of information centralization and ongoing state surveillance (Degli-Esposti & Shaikh, 2018).

6.2.3 Cyberspace and Power Contestations in Urban Development

Considering how much digital urban management systems rely on connecting citizens to those systems, the expanding internet access is a necessary step. In Southeast Asia, internet access gradually increased starting in the mid-1990s. The share of the population with internet access is unequal across countries, with the lowest penetration – below 25 percent – in Myanmar, Cambodia, Laos, and Timor-Leste, compared to 70 percent and above in Singapore, Malaysia, and Brunei as of 2015 (Lim, 2019). Big capital cities such as Bangkok, Jakarta, and Metro Manila have become social media capitals of the world, with Bangkok topping the chart for number of Facebook users and Jakarta for Twitter users by 2012 (Al Jazeera, 2012). Cyberspace has emerged as a space of social interaction, supplementing pre-existing spaces in the built environ-ment. Access to the internet is still largely concentrated in cities, however, as they are tied to infrastructure that facilitates internet penetration.

Studies by Merlyna Lim (2017; 2019) demonstrate the influence of the internet on the ways in which citizens communicate. In countries such as

Figure 8 Jakarta Smart City control room, November 2017.

Source: Author.

Indonesia and Malaysia, the Internet has facilitated communications in social movements that have called for political reforms and democratization, but the relative impact of access to cyberspace depends on sociopolitical and historical context and state–civil-society relations (Lim, 2019). While cyberspace communication can transcend city boundaries, civil society initiatives and movements remain concentrated mostly in big cities, and how much internet access matters for political change still depends on the interactions between cyberspace and other media and traditional networks (Lim, 2019).

Not only does internet access pave the way for civil society communications, but it also opens cyberspace to technocratic interventions for urban development. Forms of citizen reporting through mobile applications, such as via the reporting platform on Jakarta Smart City, allow for a more interactive relationship between city government and citizens, but entailing technocratic rather than political engagement. Mobile applications have also become platforms for market-driven responses to urban problems, such as the growth of application-based ride hailing services in various cities, with two big corporations, Gojek and Grab, originating in Southeast Asia. The state may also impose regulations on internet content, although citizens may find ways to overcome censorship. Cyberspace is neither an answer to democratization and political reform nor a solution to urban problems. Rather, cyberspace offers a platform that urban development actors can use to advance their interests and is highly likely to continue influencing future trajectories of urban development in Southeast Asia.

6.3 The Future of Civil Society Activism

The continuing significance of urban development as a purported marker of national progress suggests an important angle of inquiry into Southeast Asia's politics. Politicians' pragmatic emphasis on "real results," as they gain political capital from changes to the city, may well reduce the relationship between state actors and civil society to one resembling that between corporate producers and consumers rather than allowing democratic engagement in governance. An emphasis on visual and physical transformation to indicate progress also paves the way for government actors' alignment with private investors to enable such developments, and these investments may also affect the relationship between state and society. However, the active involvement of civil society does not diminish in these circumstances; rather, civil society maintains a political role in urban politics – as well as national politics – to varying extents in Southeast Asia.

The persistence of urban social movements for social and environmental justice, in parallel with the role of urban politicians as entrepreneurial city managers and the framing of citizens as consumers of urban services, raises at least three pertinent questions. First, if politicians become urban managers, is there still room for political life in the city? This question goes back to the primary concern raised in the first pages of this Element, of the stigmatization of dissent through the production of (beautiful) spaces as celebrations of consensus. An emphasis on convenience and comfort situates citizens as consumers and therefore limits their political role in urban development. While citizens in a democratic setting may influence levels of service delivery, infrastructure development, and other projects in the city, critical discussions regarding the negative impacts of urban development may be limited if these discussions might obstruct perceived notions of progress.

Second, if there is still room for critical discussions and debates on development projects and decisions, as well as participation of the grassroots in the city, how much does urban politics influence the political calculations of state actors? In a decentralized political system, cities can participate in the global economy more directly by welcoming investments and inviting global collaborations. But even in countries whose political systems are relatively more centralized, such as Cambodia, Laos, and Myanmar, regional and global networks of cities provide platforms for urban politicians to reach beyond national borders. The ASEAN Smart City Network is one example through which city governments can look directly for private-sector providers and financial institutions to fund initiatives. The region also has an ASEAN Mayors' Forum, which was established in 2011 and has met biannually since then, as a platform for discussions "among ASEAN's local political leaders, national policy makers, international development partners and other experts, on how cities and local governments can collaborate in the priority areas set forth for ASEAN's [Sustainable Development Goals] implementation as well as other relevant frameworks to address urbanization challenges" (UCLG-ASPAC, 2019). Moreover, Southeast Asian mayors also participate in global platforms such as the United Cities and Local Governments (UCLG) that facilitate intercity collaborations and agreements. These networking platforms do not directly imply regional or global power; rather, they are opportunities for urban politicians to showcase their achievements and gain exposure beyond their immediate administrative boundaries. These networks can potentially contribute to mayors' political capital as they may secure global and regional endorsements that are not affected by the national political economy. Consequently, the arena of urban politics in Southeast Asia today reaches beyond national and regional boundaries through these platforms.

At the same time, civil society also supports regional and global networks. This leads to the third question, which is by no means the least important: To what extent are urban social movements in Southeast Asia pragmatic, and to what extent are they ideological? Continuing issues in Southeast Asia with fulfilling basic needs and providing services for marginalized groups make it challenging to separate the pragmatic and the ideological. Nevertheless, the presence of civil society networks indicates that voices and actions from civil society organizations are important aspects to be considered in Southeast Asia's urban development. Analyzing their roles and influence requires that scholars connect general observations to grounded realities, as the concerns of civil society groups reflect development's impacts on everyday life. These groups require attention as part of studies of urban development politics as their concerns and interests are diverse, their advocacy reach may be uneven, and their consistencies and capacities may vary.

6.4 Alternative Development

Despite many challenges, cities in Southeast Asia have indicated possible ways to implement new approaches to urban development. On the one hand, as highlighted previously in this Element, governments' inability to implement plans and uphold regulations cause development inconsistencies and problems. On the other hand, those same weaknesses also induce negotiations among different urban actors, not just those between for-profit developers and the government that often exacerbate environmental and social inequalities but also between government actors and civil society groups, as around social and environmental justice. As a result, cities in Southeast Asia have also become sites of opportunities for public participation in decision-making (Padawangi, 2019).

The term "alternative development" refers to urban patterns and processes that contest the commodification of urban spaces by involving citizens as active, influential agents (Friedmann, 1992). Civil society groups' course-challenging participation in urban development depends on the existence of a public sphere, a "realm of our social life in which something approaching public opinion can be formed" (Habermas, 1964: 49), as a space of communication between civil society and state actors. Studies have traced the collective efforts of civil society groups to shape the course of urban development in Southeast Asia's history, such as the aforementioned role of associations in the formation of Singapore's municipal authority (Yeoh, 1996), the role of religious associations in facilitating advocacies on local concerns such as education and housing, and even the role of traders and migrants in affecting the development of Trowulan, the capital city in the Majapahit era (around the thirteenth to the fifteenth centuries) (Perkasa, Padawangi & Farida, 2021). The tendency to dichotomize civil society and "others," though, is misleading, as civil society actors can form coalitions to participate in shaping and directing urban development.

Several notable initiatives from the region have influenced the ways in which ideal visions of urban development have departed from the usual global city-oriented images. Central to these initiatives is community organization at the grassroots in the effort to bring forth more inclusive development. In general, such initiatives include three key areas at present: 1) inclusive housing and infrastructure; 2) community-based disaster and climate change resilience; and 3) community-led financial mechanisms (Archer, 2019). A common theme of attention to marginalized groups runs through these key areas. Instead of situating marginalized groups as passive recipients of projects and services, a focus on community organizing opens possibilities for these initiatives to empower communities to address issues that may affect their own current and future situation.

In terms of housing and infrastructure, as the first key areas of community-led urban development: much community organizing focuses on addressing housing affordability, quality, and secure tenure for marginalized groups, particularly the urban poor, who are prone to displacement. Few governments in Southeast Asia, at the national or local levels, have good strategies to ensure sufficient availability of affordable housing for the rapidly urbanizing population. In most cases, cities rely on private developers for much housing construction (Kusno, 2014; Shatkin, 2004). Housing by private developers, however, tends to serve the middle- and upper-income classes through market mechanisms and is driven by the profit-making interests of the housing provider. Meanwhile, the low-income population often faces insecure land tenure, and lack of legal acknowledgement of their residency leads to their exclusion from other public programs, such as education and healthcare.

Some housing programs in the region have departed from the usual market-based provision of housing and reliance on property developers. Indonesia's Kampung Improvement Program started in the late 1960s in Jakarta, then was widely implemented in Surabaya in the 1980s, to improve infrastructure and secure tenure in older settlements in the city by involving residents in the process. *Gawad Kalinga* in the Philippines, a comparable initiative, was a collaboration with the Housing and Urban Development Coordinating Council (HUDCC) to build participatory housing and improve infrastructure together with low-income families. In Thailand, since 2003 the *Baan Mankong* upgrading program has adopted a people-driven approach to address tenure insecurity and poor living conditions (Archer, 2019). These programs are officially recognized by local governments. On one hand, the programs have drawn criticism concerning the sustainability of the efforts, further threats of displacement by market forces and gentrification, and how unequal power remains among the local community. Overall, there have been questions over the significance of such efforts for the actual empowerment of the people (see Elinoff, 2016). On the other hand, these efforts have elevated concepts of participatory and alternative development as topics for discourse across Southeast Asia, along with raising possibilities for grassroots efforts outside official channels, from communities as well as academia, to apply these concepts.

A significant network in Southeast Asia that works on participatory housing and infrastructure is the Asian Coalition for Housing Rights (ACHR), which has grown to support community organizing efforts in nineteen countries in Asia and to facilitate connections and collaborations across these communities (Archer, 2019). Related to the ACHR are the Asian Coalition for Community Action Program (ACCA) and Community Architects Network (CAN), which have connected many urban poor activists with architects across the region to work with low-income communities for housing design and improvements. Community architects in Southeast Asia are also known for their involvement with disaster-hit populations – the second key area in community-led urban development. These architects work with disaster-affected populations to build both temporary and permanent settlements, weaving/working aspects of resilience into their designs. Although the number of persons and projects, and the intensity of activities, vary across places in the region, these groups and initiatives have increasingly, as alternative voices, called for more inclusive, collaborative, and collective approaches to urban development.

Community organizing for participatory housing often requires capacity to design suitable financial mechanisms. This relates to the third area of community-led urban development, namely community-led financial mechanisms. The *Baan Mankong* initiative in Thailand, for example, is managed by the Community Organization Development Institute (CODI), which covers community initiatives that support participatory housing. Related initiatives include organizing savings groups and participatory mapping. In other places, an initial external grant may catalyze a "rolling fund" for home improvements (Archer, 2012). This mechanism allows families to borrow funds for house renovation with a specified schedule for payback, to allow other families to subsequently utilize the scheme. This arrangement requires community organizing to decide on the mechanism and to agree on borrowing and payback rules. There are no guarantees that these financial mechanisms will work, however, as different communities may have different capacities and face different challenges. Nevertheless, the idea of self-organized, self-financed, and cooperative financial mechanisms offers a potentially workable alternative to top-down, corporate-driven investments that rely on big investors and governments.

All these possibilities for nonstate influence rely on adequate data, much as the states' own development planning does. Some communities in Southeast Asia have conducted participatory mapping in an effort to get to know their own city and to address issues from the ground. Participatory mapping involves discussions within communities, in their neighborhoods, to identify problems to address and potentials to be harnessed (Taylor, 2019). This effort is related to the inability of governments to connect with ground realities and plan accordingly. Participatory mapping is a learning process that allows for knowledge exchange between communities and researchers with a limited grasp of the local context. The result can be informative for both communities and researchers as long as there is sufficient trust that the data will be put to good use (Patel, Baptist & d'Cruz, 2012; Padawangi et al., 2016). Explains Archer: "The mapping process can identify existing infrastructure and potential hazards . . . and enables a collective gathering around a common goal" (2019: 462). The unavailability of reliable official data, government reliance on external consultants who are unfamiliar with everyday lived realities, and state officials' lack of capacity to devise and implement suitable methods to grasp the fluidity, flexibility, hybridity, and informality of urban societies are reasons to consider participatory mapping as a possible tool for aligning plans with realities.

7 Epilogue

Southeast Asia remains a rapidly urbanizing region overall, and profit-driven, large-scale, corporate-funded projects are still growing in many cities. This Element examines this region's urban development to offer a new vantage point that makes sense of various historical layers, contemporary contexts and trajectories, and possibilities for the future. It argues for the importance of grounded perspectives to recognize the role of human agency, to understand the city as a political space, and to address development injustices.

Amidst technocratic and investment-driven official narratives, alternative development initiatives are growing. Some of these alternative development programs, such as *Baan Mankong, Gawad Kalinga*, and new iterations of Indonesia's Kampung Improvement Program, have become official government programs, despite their limitations and shortcomings. Such alternatives are possible because of available space for actors from civil society, at least in neighborhoods, to discuss urban problems and potentials in the context of widespread perceptions of governments' lack of capacity. In places where the government is seen as relatively capable of delivering services, such as

Singapore, incentives and spaces to pursue alternative development initiatives may be more limited, but these initiatives are still not impossible. And voices from civil society continue to engage on issues such as heritage, environment, and food security, albeit with different degrees of influence and achievements. These voices and possibilities are only fathomable through groundedness, both in studies of and approaches to urban development.

The worldwide COVID-19 pandemic further highlights the importance of groundedness in studying urban development in Southeast Asia. On the one hand, the pandemic has paved the way for nation-states to impose top-down restrictions on social and economic activities. Requirements for social distancing have also made it difficult for civil society groups to congregate, let alone to organize for consolidated social movements. On the other hand, government control over the pandemic's spread has varied from one country to another: while Singapore and Vietnam have managed top-down control, others such as Indonesia and the Philippines have grappled with uncontrolled community spread. Here and elsewhere, the exposed weakness of the government has sparked initiatives from local communities, including self-managed neighborhood quarantines, food sharing, alternative supply chains from the countryside, crowdfunding for local needs, and collective farming, demonstrating a range of responses that can only be comprehended through a grounded perspective (Padawangi, 2022).

At least three important areas remain key for studies of urban development in Southeast Asia. First, deeper research into urban history and the multiple layers of urban development over time would contribute to a better understanding of urbanization and its political processes. For example, historical perspectives can trace patterns of migration and the roots of urban segregation to inform contemporary policies. Historical data can also be part of documenting patterns of disasters, such as flooding or earthquakes, in order to inform planning for urban resilience, drawing not just from official documents and policymakers but also from community-based perspectives. Second, urban development studies need a continuing focus on social and environmental justice, with the awareness that development can be both a cause that exacerbates as well as an answer to alleviate social and political inequality. A focus on justice would provide a base of knowledge with which to eventually shape urban politics and policies to address the issue beyond the usual grants and subsidies for the poor, instead including also empowerment of marginalized groups. Third, studies of urban development in Southeast Asia need more attention to, and suitable methods to examine, alternative development initiatives, programs, and projects, in terms of documentation of their background and current practices and in terms of their impacts. This structured evaluation is necessary if these alternatives are to become options to counterbalance the technocratic and big investment-driven development that currently dominates the pursuit of global city status.

Grappling with all three areas – historical context, social inequality, and alternative development – requires critical perspectives to ensure scholars make meaningful contributions to studies of urban development in Southeast Asia. Studying urban development is an effort to build knowledge in an area that is dominated by powerful interests in global and local economies. Therefore, the practice requires a consistently critical and analytical lens. Furthermore, the importance of urban politics beyond the city level, given networks and issues that reach to national and global levels, also poses a challenge, as scholars are continuously lured into political camps. Knowledge and information are powerful tools "for those who collect, retain, and thus control it" (ACHR, 2004: 17; Archer, 2019). Hence, critical perspectives on all actors and processes involved – from governments to the private sector, and from professionals to communities – are important to maintain in analyzing urban development. "Besides strengthening movements," Mayer notes, "groundedness in empirical realities" and attention to those who are marginalized in neoliberal urban development regimes are "preconditions for our research" (2020: 47). Remaining always grounded can help scholars to avoid perpetuating the "othering" of marginalized groups in urban development, especially if they maintain a good grasp of research methods and devise appropriate innovations when traditional research methods prove insufficient.

Urban development in Southeast Asia reflects a sense of human agency (Goh, 2018), through which social actions that challenge dominant structures and development trajectories are still possible. Studying urban development in this region is not only a matter of documenting and analyzing the situation but is also part of that exercise of human agency. As urban development studies continue to be sources of information and to offer conceptual frameworks for both official and nonofficial urban interventions, scholars who are involved in the effort directly and indirectly become part of those interventions. Southeast Asia's urban development tells us that there is much room for engaged scholarship, in which scholars immerse themselves in the field to make sense of data through actual experience, rather than accepting official, formal information as given. In the process, civil society networks may be important in finding linkages among concerns as well as identifying topics that need further inquiry. It is pertinent for urban studies scholars to be aware of their own roles in what they are studying and to understand the consequences for their subjects of their perspectives and methods.

References

ACCA (Asian Coalition for Community Action). (2014). *215 cities in Asia: Fifth yearly report of the Asian Coalition for Community Action Program*. www .achr.net/upload/files/1%20ACCA%20How%20it%20works%201–4.pdf.

ACHR (Asian Coalition for Housing Rights). (2004). Negotiating the right to stay in the city. *Environment and Urbanization* 16(1), 9–26.

Al Jazeera. (2012). Jakarta is world's most active Twitter city. www .aljazeera.com/news/asia-pacific/2012/08/201281141334716.html.

Allwinkle, S., & Cruickshank, P. (2011). Creating smart-er cities: An overview. *Journal of Urban Technology* 18(2), 1–16.

Andapita, V. (2019). "Choo choo!" Greater Jakarta on track to getting reliable rail-based public transportation. *Jakarta Post*, November 17, 2019. www .thejakartapost.com/news/2019/11/17/choo-choo-greater-jakarta-on-trackto-getting-reliable-rail-based-public-transportation.html?src=mostviewed&pg=/.

Anderson, B. (1983). *Imagined communities: Reflections on the origin and spread of nationalism*. Verso.

Antara News. (2019). Indonesia masih butuhkan pembangkit listrik batu bara. *Antaranews.com*. www.antaranews.com/berita/955478/indonesia-masih-butuhkan-pembangkit-listrik-batu-bara.

Appadurai, A. (2004). The capacity to aspire: Culture and terms of recognition. In V. Rao & M. Walton (eds.), *Culture and public action* (pp. 59–84). Stanford University Press.

Archer, D. (2012). Finance as the key to unlocking community potential: Savings, funds and the ACCA programme. *Environment and Urbanization* 24(2), 423–440.

Archer, D. (2019). Community-led processes for inclusive urban development. In R. Padawangi (ed.), *Routledge handbook of urbanization in Southeast Asia* (pp. 459–468). Routledge.

ASCN (ASEAN Smart Cities Network). (2018). *ASEAN Smart Cities Network*. Centre for Liveable Cities and Ministry of Foreign Affairs Singapore.

Baas, M. (2019). Longing and belonging in a global city: Skilled migrants in Singaporean urban space. In R. Padawangi (ed.), *Routledge handbook of urbanization in Southeast Asia* (pp. 135–145). Routledge.

Batubara, B., Warsilah, H., Wagner, I., Salam, S., & Koalisi Pesisir Semarang-Demak. (2020). *Maleh dadi Segoro: Krisis Sosial-Ekologis Kawasan Pesisir*

Semarang-Demak [*Becoming sea: social-ecological crisis in Semarang-Demak Coast*]. Lintas Nalar.

Bayat, A. (2012). Politics in the city, inside-out. *City & Society* 24(2), 110–128.

Bello, W. (2016). High-speed growth, crisis and opportunity in East Asia. In M. G. Schechter (ed.), *Future multilateralism: The political and social framework* (pp. 196–252). Springer.

Bloomberg. (2017). Move over tech: Here come Southeast Asia's builders. *Bloomberg News*. www.bloomberg.com/news/articles/2017-12-06/move-over-tech-southeast-asian-builders-come-in-focus-in-2018.

Budianta, M. (2003). The blessed tragedy: The making of women's activism during the *Reformasi* years. In A. Heryanto & S. K. Mandal (eds.), *Challenging authoritarianism in Southeast Asia: Comparing Indonesia and Malaysia* (pp. 145–177). Routledge Curzon.

Bunnell, T. (2018). Introduction: Futurity and urban Asias. In T. Bunnell & D. P. S. Goh (eds.), *Urban Asias: Essays on futurity past and present* (pp. 9–20). Jovis.

Bunnell, T., & Goh, D. P. S. (2012). Urban aspirations and Asian cosmopolitanisms. *Geoforum* 43(1), 1–3.

Bunnell, T., Goh, D. P. S., & Ng, H. (2019). Aspiration in urban(izing) Southeast Asia. In R. Padawangi (ed.), *Routledge handbook of urbanization in Southeast Asia* (pp. 115–129). Routledge.

Cairns, S. (2019). Debilitating city-centricity: Urbanization and urban-rural hybridity in Southeast Asia. In R. Padawangi (ed.), *Routledge handbook of urbanization in Southeast Asia* (pp. 288–306). Routledge.

Chalana, M., & Hou, J. (eds.) (2016). *Messy urbanism: Understanding the "other" cities of Asia*. Hong Kong University Press.

Chalermpong, S. (2019). Transportation development and urbanization in the Bangkok metropolitan region. In R. Padawangi (ed.), *Routledge handbook of urbanization in Southeast Asia* (pp. 288–306). Routledge.

Degli-Esposti, S., & Ahmed Shaikh, S. (2018). With smart cities, your every step will be recorded. *The Conversation*. https://theconversation.com/with-smart-cities-your-every-step-will-be-recorded-94527.

Department of Statistics Singapore. (2020). *Understanding age-specific fertility rate and total fertility rate*. www.singstat.gov.sg/modules/infographics/total-fertility-rate.

Dick, H., & Rimmer, P. J. (1998). Beyond the third world city: The new urban geography of South-East Asia. *Urban Studies* 35(12), 2303–2321.

DiGregorio, M. (2015). Bargaining with disaster: Flooding, climate change and urban growth ambitions in Quy Nhon City, Vietnam. *Pacific Affairs* 88(3), 577–598.

Douglass, M. (2010). Globalization, mega-projects and the environment: Urban form and water in Jakarta. *Environment and Urbanization Asia* 1(1), 45–65.

Douglass, M., & Jones, G. W. (2008). The morphology of mega-urban regions expansion. In G. W. Jones & M. Douglass (eds.), *Mega-urban regions in Pacific Asia: Urban dynamics in a global era* (pp. 19–40). NUS Press.

Douglass, M., & Jones, G. W. (2008). Mega-urban region dynamics in comparative perspective. In G. W. Jones & M. Douglass (Eds.), *Mega-urban regions in Pacific Asia: Urban dynamics in a global era* (pp. 320–349). NUS Press.

Dovey, K. (2014). Incremental urbanism: The emergence of informal settlements. In T. Haas & K. Olsson (Eds.), *Emergent Urbanism* (pp. 45–54). Ashgate.

Elinoff, E. (2016). A house is more than a house: Aesthetic politics in a northeastern Thai railway settlement. *Journal of the Royal Anthropological Institute* 22(3), 610–632.

Elinoff, E. (2018). No future here: Urbanization and hope in Thailand. In T. Bunnell & D. P. S. Goh (eds.), *Urban Asias: Essays on futurity past and present* (pp. 121–134). Jovis.

Ferzacca, S. (2022). Heritage and a community of belonging in Singapore. In M. Herzfeld & R. Padawangi (eds.), *The resilience of the vernacular: Selected case studies from Asian countries*. Amsterdam University Press.

Flanagan, M. A. (2002). *Seeing with their hearts: Chicago women and the vision of the good city 1871–1933*. Princeton University Press.

Florida, R. (2005). *The flight of the creative class: The new global competition for talent*. HarperCollins.

Forbes, D. (2019). Knowledge, creativity and the city. In R. Padawangi (ed.), *Routledge handbook of urbanization in Southeast Asia* (pp. 43–53). Routledge.

Ford, M. (2008). Women's labor activism in Indonesia. *Signs* 33(3), 510–515.

Foucault, M. (1975). *Discipline and punish: The birth of the prison*. Random House.

Friedmann, J. (1992). *Empowerment: The politics of alternative development*. Blackwell.

Gani, E. (2018). Answering Jakarta: My step to move on. Postgraduate research at the London School of Economics. https://medium.com/@edbert.gani/answering-jakarta-my-step-to-move-on-a27e91b48785.

Ghertner, D. A. (2010). Rule by aesthetics: World-class city making in Delhi. Doctoral dissertation/University of California at Berkeley. Energy and Resources, Graduate Division.

Goffman, E. (1959). *The presentation of self in everyday life*. Doubleday.

Goh, D. P. S. (2018). Conclusion: Reflections on urban agency. In T. Bunnell & D. P. S. Goh (eds.), *Urban Asias: Essays on futurity past and present* (pp. 305–310). Jovis.

Goh, D. P. S., Bunnell, T., & van der Veer, P. (2015). Introduction: Doing Asian cities. *Ethnography* 16(3), 287–294.

Habermas, J. (1964). The public sphere: An encyclopaedia article. *New German Critique* 3, 49–55.

Harms, E. (2012). Beauty as control in the New Saigon: Eviction, new urban zones, and atomized dissent in a Southeast Asian city. *American Ethnologist* 39(4), 735–750.

Harvey, D. (1973). *Social justice and the city*. Blackwell.

Harvey, D. (2003). The right to the city. *International Journal of Urban and Regional Research* 27(4), 939–941.

Hatley, B. (2002). Literature, mythology and regime change: Some observations on recent Indonesian women's writing. In K. Robinson & S. Bessell (eds.), *Women in Indonesia: Gender, equity and development* (pp. 130–143). ISEAS.

Henschke, R. (2020). Indonesia's new capital. *BBC News Global Business*. www.bbc.co.uk/programmes/w3csy82r.

Henschke, R., & Utama, A. (2020). When your capital is sinking . . . Start again? *BBC News*. www.bbc.co.uk/news/extra/xsyGF2fhsL/Indonesia_new_capital?fbclid=IwAR1FsEkS0MI1dUWP_9ulBFxjPTQ8E1T_Q7AlbaR9x-BPToZoa8torjCdIuA.

Herlambang, S., Leitner, H., Liong J. T., Sheppard, E., & Anguelov, D. (2019). Jakarta's great land transformation: Hybrid neoliberalisation and informality. *Urban Studies* 56(4), 627–648.

Hettne, B. (1995). *Development theory and the three worlds: Towards an international political economy of development* (2nd ed.). Longman Scientific & Technical.

Hollands, R. G. (2008). Will the real smart city please stand up? *City* 12(3), 303–320.

ILO (International Labour Organization). (2019). *Informal economy in Asia and the Pacific*. www.ilo.org/asia/areas/informal-economy/lang–en/index.htm.

ISEAS (Institute of Southeast Asian Studies). (2009). *Urbanisation in Southeast Asian Countries*. ISEAS.

IQAir. (2018). *2018 world air quality report: Region & city PM 2.5 ranking*. IQAir AirVisual.

Jackson, P. A. (2001). Pre-gay, post-queer: Thai perspectives on proliferating gender/sex diversity in Asia. *Journal of Homosexuality* 40(3–4), 1–25.

Jakarta Open Data (2018). *Data Angka Kelahiran, Kematian, Dan Harapan Hidup Di DKI Jakarta* [*Births, deaths, and life expectancy data in DKI Jakarta*]. https://data.jakarta.go.id/dataset/angkakelahirankematiandanh arapanhidupdidkijakarta18mei.

Johnson, H., & Simonette, V. (2019). *Lives lived and lost along Manila's Pasig River.* BBC News. www.bbc.com/news/world-asia-49203752.

Jones, G. W. (2019). Some conceptual and methodological issues in studying urbanization in Southeast Asia. In R. Padawangi (ed.), *Routledge handbook of urbanization in Southeast Asia* (pp. 90–100). Routledge.

Jones, G. W., & Douglass, M. (2008). Introduction. In G. W. Jones & M. Douglass (eds.), *Mega-urban regions in Pacific Asia: Urban dynamics in a global era* (pp. 1–18). NUS Press.

Kathiravelu, L., & Wong, G. (2019). Marginalized migrants and urbanization in Southeast Asia. In R. Padawangi (ed.), *Routledge handbook of urbanization in Southeast Asia* (pp. 146–156). Routledge.

Kenny, P. D. (2019). *Populism in Southeast Asia.* Cambridge University Press.

Kim, K., & Bui, L. (2019). An assessment of disaster risk and resilience in rapidly urbanizing ASEAN cities. In R. Padawangi (ed.), *Routledge handbook of urbanization in Southeast Asia* (pp. 325–344). Routledge.

Kitchin, R. (2014). The real-time city? Big data and smart urbanism. *GeoJournal* (79), 1–14.

Koh, S. Y. (2019). Challenges and opportunities of comparative urbanism: The case of Brunei-Miri and Singapore-Iskandar Malaysia. In R. Padawangi (ed.), *Routledge handbook of urbanization in Southeast Asia* (pp. 101–114). Routledge.

Komninos, N. (2002). *Intelligent cities: Innovation, knowledge systems and digital spaces.* Spon Press.

Kong, L. (2007). Cultural icons and urban development in Asia: Economic imperative, national identity, and global city status. *Political Geography* 26, 383–404.

Kusno, A. (2014). *After the New Order.* University of Hawaii Press.

Kusno, A. (2017a). Southeast Asia: Colonial Discourses. In C. Hein (ed.), *Routledge handbook of planning history* (pp. 218–229). Routledge.

Kusno, A. (2017b). Postcolonial Southeast Asia. In C. Hein (ed.), *Routledge Handbook of Planning History* (pp. 230–243). Routledge.

Kusno, A. (2019). Provisional notes on semi-urbanism. In R. Padawangi (ed.), *Routledge handbook of urbanization in Southeast Asia* (pp. 75–89). Routledge.

Lee, J. T-T. (2015). We built this city: Public participation in land use decisions in Singapore. *Asian Journal of Comparative Law* 10(2), 213–234.

Lim, M. (2019). Disciplining dissent: Freedom, control and digital activism in Southeast Asia. In R. Padawangi (ed.), *Routledge handbook of urbanization in Southeast Asia* (pp. 478–494). Routledge.

Lim, M. (2017). Freedom to hate: Social media, algorithmic enclaves, and the rise of tribal nationalism in Indonesia. *Critical Asian Studies* 49(3), 411–427.

Lindquist, J. (2008). *The anxieties of mobility: Migration and tourism in the Indonesian borderlands*. University of Hawaii Press.

Lombard, D. (1995). Networks and Synchronisms in Southeast Asian History. *Journal of Southeast Asian Studies* 26(1), 10–16.

Losiri, C., Nagai, M., Ninsawat, S., & Shrestha, R. P. (2016). Modeling urban expansion in Bangkok Metropolitan Region using demographic-economic data through Cellular Automata-Markov Chain and Multi-Layer Perceptron-Markov Chain models. *Sustainability* 8(7), 686.

LTA (Land Transport Authority). (2020). *Statistics*. www.lta.gov.sg/content/ltagov/en/who_we_are/statistics_and_publications/statistics.html.

Marks, D. (2019). The political ecology of uneven development and vulnerability. In R. Padawangi (ed.), *Routledge handbook of urbanization in Southeast Asia* (pp. 345–354). Routledge.

Marks, D., & Zhang, J. (2018). Circuits of power: Environmental injustice from Bangkok's shopping malls to Laos' hydropower dams. *Asia Pacific Viewpoint* 60(3), 296–309.

Matejowsky, T., & Milgram, B. L. (2019). Informality, advocacy, and governmentality in urbanizing Northern Philippine cities: Baguio, Benguet and Dagupan, Pangasinan. In R. Padawangi (ed.), *Routledge handbook of urbanization in Southeast Asia* (pp. 433–446). Routledge.

Mayer, M. (2020). What does it mean to be a (radical) urban scholar-activist, or activist-scholar, today? *City* 24(1–2), 35–51.

McGee, T. G. (2002). Reconstructing the Southeast Asian City in an era of volatile globalization. *Asian Journal of Social Science* 30(1), 8–27.

McGee, T. G. (1991). The emergence of *desakota* regions in Asia: Expanding a hypothesis. In N. Ginsburg, B. M. Koppel & T. G. McGee (eds.), *The extended metropolis: Settlement transition in Asia* (pp. 3–25). University of Hawai'i Press.

McGee, T. G. (1967). *The Southeast Asian city: Between modernity and development*. Routledge.

McGee, T. G., & Shaharudin, I. (2016). Reimagining the "peri-urban" in the mega-urban regions of Southeast Asia. In B. Maheshwari, V. P. Singh & B. Thoradeniya (eds.), *Balanced urban development: Options and strategies for liveable cities* (pp. 499–516). Springer.

MDHS (Myanmar Demographic and Health Survey) (2015–16). *Key Indicators*. https://reliefweb.int/sites/reliefweb.int/files/resources/MDHS% 202015-16%20KIR.pdf.

Mills, M. B. (2005). From nimble fingers to raised fists: Women and labor activism in globalizing Thailand. *Signs* 31(1), 117–144.

Ministry of Health and Lao Statistics Bureau (2012). *Lao Social Indicator Survey 2011–12*. Vientiane, Lao PDR.

The Nation. (2018). The "Battery of Asia" could face a short-circuit. Editorial note, August 15, 2018. www.straitstimes.com/asia/se-asia/the-battery-of-asia-could-face-a-short-circuit-the-nation.

National Population and Family Planning Board (BKKBN), Statistics Indonesia (BPS), Ministry of Health (Kemenkes), & ICF (2018). *Indonesia Demographic and Health Survey 2017*. BKKBN, BPS, Kemenkes, and ICF.

Nature Society (2020). *History & Accomplishments*. www.nss.org.sg/about .aspx?id=2.

Norris, C. (2005). From personal to digital: CCTV, the panopticon, and the technological mediation of suspicion and social control. In *Surveillance as Social Sorting* (pp. 263–295). Routledge.

Oetomo, D. (2008). Claiming gay persons' sexual rights in Indonesia. *Sexual Health Exchange 2001–3*. www.kit.nl/exchange/html/2001-3-claiming_ gay_persons.asp.

Ong, A., & Peletz, M. G. (1995). Introduction. In A. Ong & M. G. Peletz (eds.), *Bewitching women, pious men: Gender and body politics in Southeast Asia* (pp. 1–18). University of California Press.

Ortega, A. A. C. (2019). Mega-regionalization of a nation: Philippine mega-regions and the impulse to globalize. In R. Padawangi (ed.), *Routledge handbook of urbanization in Southeast Asia* (pp. 207–220). Routledge.

Padawangi, R. (2014). Reform, resistance and empowerment: Constructing the public city from the grassroots in Jakarta, Indonesia. *International Development Planning Review* 36(1), 33–50.

Padawangi, R. (2018a). In search of alternative development in post-*Reformasi* Jakarta. In J. Hellman, M. Thynell & R. van Voorst (eds.), *Jakarta: Claiming spaces and rights in the city* (pp. 173–194). Routledge.

Padawangi, R. (2018b). The social city: Aspiration of an urban transformation in Asia. Friedrich Ebert Stiftung Discussion Paper. https://library.fes.de/pdf-files/bueros/indonesien/14364-20180429.pdf.

Padawangi, R. (2018c). Excavating the ruins of aspirational urban futures in Bukit Duri, Jakarta. In T. Bunnell & D. P. S. Goh (eds.), *Urban Asias: Essays on futurity past and present* (pp. 205–208). Jovis.

Padawangi, R. (2019). Forced evictions, spatial (un)certainties and the making of exemplary centres in Indonesia. *Asia Pacific Viewpoint* 60(1), 65–79.

Padawangi, R. (2020). Questioning Normalcy: Rethinking Urbanisation, Development and Collective Action through the COVID-19 Moment. *LSE-SEAC Blog*. https://blogs.lse.ac.uk/seac/2020/07/20/questioning-normalcy-rethinking-urbanisation-development-and-collective-action-through-the-covid-19-moment/.

Padawangi, R., & Vallée, M. (2017). Water connections: Output-Based Aid for the urban poor and the pursuit of water justice in Jakarta, Indonesia. In B. Caniglia, M. Vallée & B. Frank (eds.), *Resilience, Environmental Justice and the City* (pp. 118–137). Routledge.

Padawangi, R. (2016). Benedict Anderson: A reflection by an Indonesian urbanist. *Theory, Culture and Society* 33(7–8), 329–333.

Padawangi, R., Rabé, P., & Perkasa, A. (2021). River cities: Water space in urban development and history. In R. Padawangi, P. Rabé & A. Perkasa (eds.) *River Cities: Water space in urban development and history*. Amsterdam University Press.

Padawangi, R., Turpin, E., Herlily, Prescott, M.F., Lee, I., & Shepherd, A. (2016). Mapping an alternative community river: The case of the Ciliwung. *Sustainable Cities and Society* (20), 147–157.

Padawangi, R., & Douglass, M. (2015). Water, water everywhere: Toward participatory solutions to chronic urban flooding in Jakarta. *Pacific Affairs* 88(3), 517–550.

Paddison, R. (2009). Some reflections on the limitations to public participation in the post-political city. *L'Espace Politique* 8. https://journals.openedition.org/espacepolitique/1393.

Patel, S., Baptist, C., & d'Cruz, C. (2012). Knowledge is power: Informal communities assert their right to the city through SDI and community-led enumerations. *Environment and Urbanization* 24(1), 13–26.

Peeters, R. (2013). *Surabaya, 1945–2010: Neighbourhood, state and economy in Indonesia's city of struggle*. NUS Press.

Perkasa, A. (2012). *Orang-orang Tionghoa dan Islam di Majapahit* [The Chinese and Islam in Majapahit]. Ombak.

Perkasa, A., Padawangi, R., & Farida, E. N. (2021). *Bhinneka Tunggal Ika*: From slogan to everyday urban? Examining neighborhood practices of diversity as counter-discourse in Kampung Peneleh, Surabaya. *Building City Knowledge from Neighborhoods*. Asia Research Institute, Singapore.

Phuc, N. Q., Zoomers, A., & van Westen, A. C. M. (2015). Compulsory land acquisition for urban expansion: A study of farmer's protest in peri-urban Hue, Central Vietnam. Conference: Land grabbing, conflict and agrarian-environmental transformations: Perspectives from East and Southeast Asia (June 5–6, 2015), Conference Paper No. 59.

Kojima, M., Iwasaki, F., Johannes, H. P., & Edita, E. P. (2020). Policy Brief: Strengthening waste management policies to mitigate the COVID-19 pandemic. *Economic research Institute for ASEAN and East Asia (ERIA)*. www .think-asia.org/bitstream/handle/11540/12206/Strengthening-Waste-Management-Policies-to-Mitigate-the-COVID19-Pandemic-.pdf.

Preecharushh, D. (2010). Myanmar's new capital city of Naypyidaw. In S. D. Brunn (ed.), *Engineering Earth* (pp. 1021–1044). Springer.

Pujiwati & Upik. (2007). Pengantar: Menjadi ibu rumah tangga yang memahami hak-hak ekonomi, sosial, dan budaya [Introduction: becoming a housewife with awareness on economic, social, and cultural rights]. In A. A. Ratih, M. Fauzi & S. Setyosiswanto (eds.), *Di antara belantara Jakarta: Pengalaman kaum ibu di Rempoa dan Cilandak Barat [Amid the concrete jungle of Jakarta: experiences of women in Rempoa and West Cilandak]* (pp. 1–24). Suara Ibu Peduli and Elkasa.

Philippine Statistics Authority (PSA) and ICF International. (2014). *Philippines National Demographic and Health Survey 2013*. PSA and ICF International.

Reid, A. (1993). *Southeast Asia in the age of commerce, 1450–1680: Volume 2, Expansion and crisis*. Yale University Press.

Rimmer, P. J., & Dick, H. (2019). Gateways, corridors and peripheries. In R. Padawangi (ed.), *Routledge handbook of urbanization in Southeast Asia* (pp. 9–30). Routledge.

Rimmer, P. J., & Dick, H. (2009). *The city in Southeast Asia: Patterns, Processes and Policy*. NUS Press.

Roberts, J. L. (2019). In search of urban identities in Myanmar. In R. Padawangi (Ed.), *Routledge handbook of urbanization in Southeast Asia* (pp. 400–410). Routledge.

Roy, A. (2009). Why India cannot plan its cities: Informality, Insurgence and the idiom of urbanization. *Planning Theory* 8(1), 76–87.

Rukmana, D. (2015). The change and transformation of Indonesian spatial planning after Suharto's New Order regime: The case of the Jakarta Metropolitan Area. *International Planning Studies* 20(4), 1–21.

Salim, W., Hudalah, D., & Firman, T. (2018). Spatial planning and urban development in Jakarta's metropolitan area. In J. Hellman, M. Thynell & R. van Voorst (eds.), *Jakarta: Claiming spaces and rights in the city* (pp. 58–74). Routledge.

Sarkar, S., & De, E. N. (2002). Introduction: Marking times and territories. In S. Sarkar & E. N. De (eds.), *Trans-Status Subjects: Gender in the Globalization of South and Southeast Asia* (pp. 1–29). Duke University Press.

Savage, V. R. (2019). The urban transformation in Southeast Asia: From cosmic cities to urban centers. In R. Padawangi (ed.), *Routledge handbook of urbanization in Southeast Asia* (pp. 375–386). Routledge.

Savirani, A., & Aspinall, E. (2017). Adversarial linkages: The urban poor and electoral politics in Jakarta. *Journal of Current Southeast Asian Affairs* 36(3), 3–34.

Sereypagna, P. (2018). A genealogy of Phnom Penh's white building: From modern minimal housing unit to reimagining of alternative urban futures. In T. Bunnell & D. P. S. Goh (eds.), *Urban Asias: Essays on futurity past and present* (pp. 43–54). Jovis.

Shatkin, G. (2004). Planning to forget: Informal settlements as "forgotten places" in globalising Metro Manila. *Urban Studies* 41(12), 2469–2484.

Silas, J. (2020). *Johan Silas: Kekhasan kota ada di kampungnya* [Johan Silas: a city's uniqueness is in its kampungs]. *Tempo Magazine.* https://majalah.tempo.co/read/lingkungan/159759/cerita-tokoh-arsitektur-johan-silas-soal-konsep-kota-kampung-surabaya?hidden=login.

Simmel, G. (1903). *The metropolis and mental life*. Blackwell.

Simone, A. M. (2019). The politics of increments in collective urban action. In R. Padawangi (ed.), *Routledge handbook of urbanization in Southeast Asia* (pp. 64–74). Routledge.

Simone, A. M. (2014). *Jakarta: Drawing the city near*. University of Minnesota Press.

Simone, A. M., & Pieterese, E. J. (2017). *New urban worlds: Inhabiting dissonant times*. Wiley.

Singapore Government (2019). *The planning act: Master plan written statement 2019*. www.ura.gov.sg/-/media/Corporate/Planning/Master-Plan/MP19writtenstatement.pdf?la=en.

Sinha, V. (2018). Methodological musings: Trawling Singapore's urban religious landscapes. In T. Bunnell & D. P. S. Goh (eds.), *Urban Asias: Essays on futurity past and present* (pp. 263–276). Jovis.

Siswanto & Raharjo, D. B. (2016). Reklamasi Pulau G lanjut, Ahok kebut rusun dari duit pengembang [Islet G reclamation continues, Ahok speeds up development of rental flats using money from private developers]. *Suara.com*, September 13, 2016. www.suara.com/news/2016/09/13/221451/reklamasi-pulau-g-lanjut-ahok-kebut-rusun-dari-duit-pengembang.

Steinberg, F. (2007). Jakarta: Environmental problems and sustainability. *Habitat International* 31, 354–365.

Stoler, A. L. (2008). Imperial debris: Reflections on ruins and ruination. *Cultural Anthropology* 23(2), 191–219.

Sutherland, H. (1974). Notes on Java's regent families: Part II. *Indonesia* 17, 1–42.

Taylor, J. (2019). Citywide participatory community mapping. In R. Padawangi (ed.), *Routledge handbook of urbanization in Southeast Asia* (pp. 469–477). Routledge.

Tonkiss, F. (2005). *Space, the city and social theory: Social relations and urban forms*. Polity Press.

Tran, H. A. (2019). From socialist modernism to market modernism? Master-planned developments in post-reform Vietnam. In R. Padawangi (ed.), *Routledge handbook of urbanization in Southeast Asia* (pp. 249–264). Routledge.

UCLG-ASPAC. (2019). 5th ASEAN Mayors Forum: Driving local actions for sustainable and inclusive growth (Concept Note). https://uclg-aspac.org/wp-content/uploads/2019/07/AMF_Concept-Note-1.pdf.

UKNA (Urban Knowledge Network Asia). (2020). The Southeast Asia Neighborhoods Network (SEANNET). www.ukna.asia/seannet.

UNEP (United Nations Environment Programme). (2017). *Waste management in ASEAN countries: Summary Report*. UNEP.

United Nations (2018). *The World's Cities in 2018 Data Booklet*. United Nations. www.un.org/en/events/citiesday/assets/pdf/the_worlds_cities_in_2018_data_booklet.pdf.

United Nations Human Settlement Programme (UN-Habitat). (2015). *Global urban indicators database 2015*.

United Nations Population Division. (2018). *World urbanization prospects: 2018 revision*. https://data.worldbank.org/indicator/SP.URB.TOTL.IN.ZS?end=2018&start=1960.

UPCA (Urban Poor Coalition Asia). (2012). *Declaration of commitment and action of the Urban Poor Coalition Asia*. www.achr.net/upload/downloads/file_16122013102518.pdf.

URA (Urban Redevelopment Authority Singapore). (2020a). *Concept plan*. www.ura.gov.sg/Corporate/Planning/Concept-Plan.

URA (Urban Redevelopment Authority Singapore). (2020b). *Master plan*. www.ura.gov.sg/Corporate/Planning/Master-Plan.

URA (Urban Redevelopment Authority Singapore). (2020c). *Past concept plans*. www.ura.gov.sg/Corporate/Planning/Concept-Plan/Past-Concept-Plans.

URA (Urban Redevelopment Authority Singapore). (2020d). Concept plan 2011 and MND land use plan. www.ura.gov.sg/Corporate/Planning/Concept-Plan/Land-Use-Plan.

Utomo, A. (2005). Romanticising the gender wage gap in modern Indonesia: Old themes and new ideas in labour market expectations. *International Union for the Scientific Study of the Population XXV International Population Conference Tours*.

Vollmer, D., Costa, D., Lin, E. S., Ninsalam, Y., Shaad, K., Prescott, M. F., Gurusamy, S., Remondi, F., Padawangi, R., Burlando, P., Girot, C., Grêt-Regamey, A., & Rekittke, J. (2015). Changing the course of rivers in an Asian city: Linking landscapes to human benefits through iterative modelling and design. *Journal of the American Water Resources Association* 51(3), 672–688.

Wade, G. D. (2012). Southeast Asian Islam and Southern China in the fourteenth century. In G. Wade & Li T. (eds.), *Anthony Reid and the study of Southeast Asian past* (pp. 125–145). ISEAS.

Warouw, N. (2019). Women workers and urban imagination in Indonesia's industrial town. In R. Padawangi (ed.), *Routledge handbook of urbanization in Southeast Asia* (pp. 157–167). Routledge.

Weber, Max (1921 [1986]). *The City*. The Free Press.

Wilson, I. (2011). Reconfiguring rackets: Racket regimes, protection and the state in post-New Order Jakarta. In E. Aspinall & G. van Klinken (eds.), *The state and illegality in Indonesia* (pp. 239–260). KITLV Press.

Wirth, L. (1938). Urbanism as a way of life. *American Journal of Sociology* 44(1), 1–25.

World Bank Data. (2019). *Fertility rate, total (births per woman) – Brunei Darussalam*. https://data.worldbank.org/indicator/SP.DYN.TFRT.IN? locations=BN.

Yamada, T. S. (2019). Phnom Penh's Diamond Island: City of spectacle. In R. Padawangi (ed.), *Routledge handbook of urbanization in Southeast Asia* (pp. 307–319). Routledge.

Yap, K. S. (2019). Peri-urban transformations in Southeast Asia. In R. Padawangi (ed.), *Routledge handbook of urbanization in Southeast Asia* (pp. 43–53). Routledge.

Yap, K. S., & M. Thuzar (eds.) (2012). *Urbanization in Southeast Asia: Issues and impacts*. ISEAS.

Yasmeen, G. (2002). Nurturing, gender ideologies, and Bangkok's foodscape. In S. Sarkar & E. N. De (eds.), *Trans-status subjects: Gender in the globalization of South and Southeast Asia* (pp. 147–166). Duke University Press.

Yeoh, B. S. A. (1996). *Contesting Space in Colonial Singapore*. Oxford University Press.

Yeoh, B. S. A. (2005). The global cultural city? Spatial Imagineering and politics in the (multi)cultural marketplaces of South-East Asia. *Urban Studies* 42(5–6), 945–958.

Yeoh, B. S. A., & Huang, S. (1998). Negotiating public space: strategies and styles of migrant female domestic workers in Singapore. *Urban Studies* 35(3), 583–602.

Yu, S. (2020). *Jakarta Kota Air – Part 4*. Watchdoc Documentary Maker. www .youtube.com/watch?v=zFzBc7cQHQc.

Cambridge Elements ≡

Politics and Society in Southeast Asia

Edward Aspinall

Australian National University

Edward Aspinall is a professor of politics at the Coral Bell School of Asia-Pacific Affairs, Australian National University. A specialist in Southeast Asia, especially Indonesia, much of his research has focused on democratisation, ethnic politics and civil society in Indonesia, and, most recently, clientelism across Southeast Asia.

Meredith L. Weiss

University at Albany, SUNY

Meredith L. Weiss is Professor of Political Science at the University at Albany, SUNY. Her research addresses political mobilization and contention, the politics of identity and development, and electoral politics in Southeast Asia, with particular focus on Malaysia and Singapore.

About the series

The Elements series Politics and Society in Southeast Asia includes both country-specific and thematic studies on one of the world's most dynamic regions. Each title, written by a leading scholar of that country or theme, combines a succinct, comprehensive, up-to-date overview of debates in the scholarly literature with original analysis and a clear argument.

Cambridge Elements $\equiv$

Politics and Society in Southeast Asia

A full series listing is available at: www.cambridge.org/ESEA

Printed in the United States
by Baker & Taylor Publisher Services